The Homosexual Crisis In the Mainline Church

School of Divinity

Gardner-Webb University
School of Divinity

This book donated
by

Ken Batts

The Homosexual Crisis in the Mainline Church

A Presbyterian Minister Speaks Out

by
Jerry R. Kirk

Thomas Nelson Inc., Publishers
Nashville • New York

© 1978 by Thomas Nelson, Inc.

All rights reserved under International and Pan-American Conventions. Published in Nashville, Tennessee, by Thomas Nelson Inc., Publishers and simultaneously in Don Mills, Ontario, by Thomas Nelson & Sons (Canada) Limited. Manufactured in the United States of America.

Unless otherwise indicated, all Scripture quotations are from the Revised Standard Version of the Bible, copyrighted 1946, 1952, © 1971, 1973.

Second Printing–

ISBN 0-8407-5655-0

Dedicated to

Peter Gillquist and Fritz Ridenour without whose guidance and gentle nudge this book would never have been written;

the staff, session, and members of the College Hill Presbyterian Church who are loving me into wholeness and setting me free to follow Jesus Christ with abandon; and

my wife, Patricia, and our children, Kimberly, Kari, Timothy, Kristen, and Stephen, whose lives give me strength and hope, and whose love made me secure enough to risk writing a book like this.

Contents

Preface

In January of 1976, word came that the Presbytery of New York City was seeking *definitive guidance* concerning the ordination of an avowed practicing homosexual to the gospel ministry. The request went on to say that since "a person is ordained for the whole church and the General Assembly is the final authority on matters of doctrine and the interpretation of the Constitution of the Church," the presbytery was asking the General Assembly for that *definitive guidance.*

That request caused me to struggle. I thought of many persons, men and women involved in homosexual practices with whom I had counseled and how God had opened their minds to His truth in Scripture, their hearts to the grace of Jesus Christ, and their lives to a new beginning and a different lifestyle—to a life of hope in the midst of struggle—a changed life in process of being changed even more. Concern for those people and others like them, concern for the members of College Hill Church, and concern for God's people everywhere led our session and presbytery to seek *immediate* guidance from the General Assembly—clear, compassionate, and balanced guidance that would clarify the biblical teaching that homosexual acts are sinful and that ordination without repentance and healing would be wrong.

In the months following I have come to a second conviction of equal importance to me. God is calling all of His people to face their sins more deeply than ever before and to repent of them. God gently began to show me my sins of self-righteousness, anger, and fear that were robbing me of the ability to love homosexuals. God has not made such love optional. I began to see my sin through the eyes of Jesus Christ and realized that I could not call homosexuals to repentance and new life in Christ without seeking repentance myself as well.

It is time to speak, time to learn, time to hope, and time for action.

In the truest sense this book is a team effort. Mrs. Sarah Blanken led a team of women who gave lavishly of their time and talents. Without her, this book would not have been written. Mrs. Sharlyn Stare, Mrs. Marybelle Chapman, and Mrs. Carol Loescher were close teammates in the task. Dr. Gary R. Sweeten, minister of discipleship at College Hill, gave invaluable assistance, especially in chapters eight and thirteen.

Apart from seeing and sharing in the life of our congregation through worship, loving fellowship, and the healing transforming power of Christ, this book would never have been born in my heart nor written in God's providence. He is the source of anything good in it. I am the source of all the blemishes.

Names and places of persons have been changed in order to protect them from the anguish of detection and to allow their continued growth in the freedom of the Spirit.

Jerry R. Kirk

College Hill Presbyterian Church
Cincinnati, Ohio
February, 1978

I.

A Time to Speak

1

Gay Rights
Go to Church

THE GAY CRISIS has come to church!

A young man in our church who plans to enter Pittsburgh Seminary came to me recently and said, "I'm confused. I don't understand where we are as a church. This sounds crazy, but is the United Presbyterian Church really for me? I don't know what I should do about seminary."

He is one of six young men from my congregation planning to enter seminary. What would you have said to him?

A middle-aged pastor of a large church in Pennsylvania said to me not long ago on the telephone, "If the General Assembly votes to say homosexual acts can be good and such persons can be ordained, I'll have lost my spiritual home."

Another pastor from a nearby city called the next morning. We hadn't visited together for some time.

"Hello, Jerry? This is Dick. Have you read the summary of the majority report of the Task Force on Homosexuality?"

"Yes, I have, Dick."

"I can't believe it," he said with great protest. "It's crazy. It's not only ignorant; it's stupid. Where in the world have we been? Don't we know what the Scriptures say? Don't we care what our people think any more? Doesn't it matter what this will do to the church?"

13

That led to a lengthy conversation of sharing frustration, surprise, and even anger. It also led to the expression of our deep concern for what God had to say on the matter and how the issue would affect the well-being of our church.

But all of the response was not on that side of the fence. One pastor said to me, "I believe the time has come when we need to ordain a homosexual. I believe we need to do it so that we can affirm these broken people and so that we will have leaders who can minister to this sizeable subculture in our society."

The gay crisis *has* come to church. We've seen it before on the newsstand and on television, and we've come to expect it in our culture. But now it's in the church as well.

Homosexuals have been a part of the church in the past because they, like heterosexuals, have needed and sought God's mercy and help. They have not always seen God's grace in people, although many have seen His grace in the person of Jesus Christ.

WHAT THE GAY PEOPLE ARE SAYING

Now gay people are coming to church not only for forgiveness and mercy, or for acceptance and love, but for a different reason. Their purpose is to say to the church and the world, "My gayness is good. My homosexuality is not sinful—it's okay. God made me this way. God accepts my sexuality and my lifestyle as good. It's natural to me; therefore the time has come for *you* to accept me as I am, and join with me in saying that gayness is good."

Troy Perry, a former Pentecostal preacher, began in 1968 to preach as an openly-practicing homosexual. He founded a congregation for gays which has since become the M.C.C. denomination (Metropolitan Community Church). He was impressed by these ideas:

God loves everyone, including homosexuals;
God made man in His own image;
He made homosexuals;
Therefore, homosexuality is a "gift of God";
God accepts me (Troy Perry) and my homosexuality as good;
God wants me to start a church for homosexuals.[1]

In 1968 those were startling and unbelievable ideas. Ten years later, they are held by many gays and are being promoted by many leaders and theologians within the mainline churches.

The gay theologian is calling for the church to change its understanding of the Scripture, its historic theology, and its view of sexuality and morality in its approach to man as male and female. The challenge comes, "I call upon the church to tell the world of your change of convictions by ordaining me with full knowledge of my homosexual commitment."

This is the issue before us in the mainline churches. Some will say, "Maybe we've been too narrow. Should we as a church lead the way in society by giving gays the recognition they want?" Others will respond, "This is insanity! Who in the *world*, let alone the *church*, would take these people seriously? How is it possible that such requests could even be made to those of us who are committed to the authority of Scripture?"

A BRIEF BACKGROUND

If you are asking either of these questions, you're certainly not the first to do so. Nor will you be the last. These same questions were asked by thousands of pastors and lay people within my own denomination, the United Presbyterian Church, when in 1976 the New York Presbytery asked the General Assembly to establish a task force to give "definitive guidance" to the presbytery.

Very few people took the request seriously. "Why do we need a study," they alleged, "when Scripture is so clear? No one would consider ordaining an avowed, practicing homosexual."

Numerous leaders stated to me that there was no possibility of the task force ever supporting the ordination of homosexuals. But now, two years later, that task force report has been made public, and it includes a majority decision that *does* suggest not only that gayness can be good, but that homosexuals, if qualified, can be ordained to the ministry. The unthinkable—in the minds of the vast majority of United Presbyterians—is now not only thinkable, but is being recommended for adoption at the next meeting of the General Assembly.

We United Presbyterians are not alone in facing this issue. In early 1978, a group of four United Methodist bishops indicated their openness toward the ordination of practicing homosexuals in their church. At this writing, a lesbian has received ordination in the Episcopal Church. Other church bodies—the Lutherans, the Disciples of Christ, and even the Roman Catholic Church—are facing the matter with heated debate. And the issue goes well beyond the mainline churches.

THE LINES OF DEMARCATION

We all know that in any battle it is dangerous to be in the cross fire and to linger there too long. This is especially true when the ammunition is heavy and the guns are legion. But this is where we find ourselves.

On the one side, supported by their sympathizers, are the "gay liberationists" saying, "Don't talk to us about accepting us as persons but not accepting our homosexuality as good. We can't live with that any longer. We've already suffered more than you can ever realize. If you

16

will not accept our homosexuality, then *you* are the enemy."

On the other side are those who want to end the discussion. In fact, they didn't want to begin the discussion in the first place. They're appalled that any Christian, let alone any Christian knowledgeable of the Scriptures, theology, and church history, could ever pose the question of whether or not homosexual acts are sinful. To go a step beyond and suggest that maybe such a person could be ordained to the gospel ministry is a greater shock. But to have the question asked by a presbytery, and to have the General Assembly spend $70,000 for a two-year study to "find the answer," is for most totally unbelievable.

Christians within the churches, ducking the cross fire, are looking for a clear word about homosexuality as it relates to God's truth. They want a balanced word, a word that brings together the whole view of the Scripture; they want hope as well as judgment, love and healing as well as a call for repentance. What they are looking for is not only God's evaluation of homosexuality (or of homosexual acts as sin), but how the gospel and the power of God can intervene with compassion and bring new life to the homosexual.

2

Deadlines and Dominoes

THE MAINLINE CHURCH is facing a time bomb. There is pressure from within and without not only to respond to the homosexual crisis, but to do it *now*. Gay liberationists and their sympathizers are hoping that the domino effect will be set in motion and result in support for their goals both within denominations and across denominational lines.

Most of the gay-rights leadership and the pressure producing the current gay crisis has come from New York City and San Francisco. In New York the gay movement began with the riots following the Stonewall arrests in 1969. In 1972 the first avowed male homosexual was ordained into the United Church of Christ ministry in San Francisco (where later one hundred thousand people marched for gay rights and the police department played a publicized baseball game with gay leaders). In 1977 the first ordination of a known lesbian took place in New York City by the Episcopal Church.

There have been both gains and losses, from the gay viewpoint, within these churches. In order to better understand the broad picture on gay rights and the church, let us look quickly at how the various denominations are responding to the issue.

THE UNITED CHURCH OF CHRIST

In 1972 the Golden Gate Association of the United Church of Christ ordained a self-declared homosexual, William R. Johnson. They did so in spite of the advice against it by the denomination's Council on Church and Ministry. In the United Church of Christ's polity, the local association has the right of final decision. They used that right to get things going. William Johnson has not yet served a congregation as pastor, but he has worked extensively to further gay theology and gay rights within the United Church of Christ and other denominations.

By way of contrast, in 1975 Edward Hougen, a United Church of Christ clergyman, revealed that he was a homosexual; his wife Margaret, also a minister, admitted having extramarital sexual relationships. When they moved to Boston where he became pastor of a gay church (Metropolitan Community Church), their membership in their former U.C.C. Association was revoked.

THE EPISCOPAL CHURCH

In 1977 the Right Reverend Paul Moore, Jr., Bishop of New York for the Episcopal Church, ordained Ellen Marie Barrett, an avowed lesbian, to the priesthood. She had been active in the gay movement prior to that time and served as an officer of "Integrity," the Episcopalian gay caucus.

Bishop Moore received an avalanche of protest within the Episcopal Church, both from fellow bishops and from people within his diocese. Several dioceses expressed opposition at their annual conventions. The diocese of Texas asked for Moore's removal by a nearly two-to-one margin. One magazine reported, "Across the church, storms of opposition were predominant. Presiding Bishop John M. Allen, who is decidedly less liberal than Moore, felt led to warn against excessive reaction, and assured Episcopalians that their church would not be destroyed by a single ordination."[1]

Bishop Moore expressed surprise at the response and defended himself with this theological statement:

> In briefest form, I believe that better guidance will be found in the fullness of the Gospel than in the narrowness of isolated verses selected painstakingly from the Epistles or the Old Testament. There is a timelessness to the message of God's love that outweighs the datedness of so many biblical injunctions rooted in ancient societies.[2]

Ellen Barrett is now studying in California. But the controversy continues to grow. Many congregations have left the Episcopal Church because of the ordination of women, and much unrest has developed over the homosexual issue. The House of Bishops has ruled that homosexuals should not be married in the church nor be ordained priests.[3] Bishop John Krumm, prominent bishop of southern Ohio, expressed his own disapproval of Miss Barrett's ordination and his "intention not to ordain anyone who is a self-confessed homosexual and feels obliged to admit it publicly."[4] A special study on homosexuality to be completed in 1979 is underway within the House of Bishops.

THE UNITED METHODIST CHURCH

Obvious pressure began in 1974 when the United Methodist Church's Council on Youth Ministry passed a resolution declaring that "homosexuality should not be a bar to the ministry."[5] The debate has escalated.

In 1976 the General Conference rejected the proposal of the Board of Church and Society to alter the "Social Principles" in the direction of greater acceptance of homosexuality (Part Three of *The Book of Discipline*). They also rejected a proposal to establish a four-year study of human sexuality including homosexuality. However, the delegates did not decide to ban the ordination of homosexuals, and so that issue continues to cause controversy in the local annual conferences.

The 1976 *Book of Discipline of the United Methodist Church* describes the sacred worth of all persons, including homosexuals, but then says, "Further, we insist that all persons are entitled to have their human and civil rights ensured, though we do not condone the practice of homosexuality and consider this practice incompatible with Christian teaching."[6]

THE UNITED PRESBYTERIAN CHURCH

The General Assembly of the United Presbyterian Church, meeting in May of 1978, will act on the reports of a task force that for fifteen months has been studying the issue of ordination of practicing homosexuals to the ministry. As has been noted, this study grew out of the request of the New York Presbytery for "definitive guidance from the Assembly."[7] The majority report suggests that same-sex love can be good and within the plan of God and, therefore, it would be proper for presbyteries to ordain avowed, practicing homosexuals.[8]

The report recommends putting the decision back into the hands of presbyteries. It gives specific guidance to the presbyteries, as requested by the Presbytery of New York, by saying there is nothing in the Constitution that hinders the ordination of practicing homosexuals.[9] In other words, it defines what the Constitution does not say, and in so doing opens the door for presbyteries to do whatever they decide and prepares the way for a positive response by removing all obstacles.

The minority report, in contrast to the majority report, sees homosexual acts as contrary to God's intention, that such acts are, therefore, sin. While it calls the church to be sensitive to the needs of gay persons in ministering to them, it recommends "that the General Assembly exercise its judicial role as the highest judicatory of the church . . . and determine a definitive interpretation of the Constitution which specifies that self-affirming, practicing homosexual persons may not be ordained to the professional ministry, or to the offices of ruling elder and deacon. . . ."[10]

The majority report has been endorsed by the Advisory Council on Church and Society by a twelve-to-three vote. Therefore, it comes to the Assembly from both the task force and the council. The chairperson of the council and the moderator of the Assembly had full authority and responsibility in appointing the nineteen-member task force.

The United Presbyterian Church faces a strange dilemma. It is receiving a task force report that is at sharp variance with the opinion of the overwhelming majority of its people, as evidenced by the official "Presbyterian Panel Survey of January 1977" (see Appendix 2, page 175), requested specifically by the task force itself.[11] The overwhelming majority of members, elders, pastors, and missionaries voted "no, never" or "no, probably not" to the question: "Might it ever be judicious and proper for a presbytery to ordain to the professional ministry a person who engages in homosexual activity?" Other surveys have indicated similar results.

Numerous presbyteries and church sessions are responding officially, before the General Assembly takes action, out of concern that they need to be heard. The Presbytery of Chicago is one of these. It stated by a vote of 225 to 78:

Whereas, the Scriptures and the Confessions of the Church
have declared the practice of homosexuality to be
sinful, and,
Whereas, Candidates for Ordination "shall be instructed by
the Confessions of the Church," and,
Whereas, the ordination of avowed homosexuals would re-
pudiate the Confessional Standards of the
Church,
We Move that the Presbytery of Chicago go on record as
affirming publicly the Confessions of the
Church, the 1970 and 1975 General Assemblies'
statements concerning homosexuality, and
therefore oppose the ordination of avowed, practicing homosexual persons.[12]

It also called the church to a ministry of Christ's love so
that homosexual persons would know "the liberating and
changing power of the Gospel."[13]

THE PRESBYTERIAN CHURCH IN
THE UNITED STATES

The Presbyterian Church in the United States (also
called the Southern Presbyterian Church) has developed
a very helpful study document available through the
Clerk's Office in Atlanta, Georgia. It is entitled, "The
Church and Homosexuality: A Preliminary Study."

There is great need for more adequate understanding of
homosexuality, and this study provides it. In endorsing
this document for study throughout the Presbyterian
Church in the United States, the 1977 General Assembly
also stated, "Although we confess our need for more light
and pray for spiritual guidance for the Church on this
matter, we now believe that homosexuality falls short of
God's plan for sexual relationships and urge the Church to
seek the best ways for witnessing to God's moral stan-

dards and for ministering to homosexual persons concerning the love of God in Jesus Christ."[14]

THE SOUTHERN BAPTIST CONVENTION

The Southern Baptist Convention adopted their first resolution on homosexuality in 1976. It urged local congregations "not to afford the practice of homosexuality any degree of approval through ordination, employment, or other designations of a normal lifestyle." [15]

EASTERN ORTHODOX CHURCHES

The Orthodox also have strongly rejected the idea of ordination of homosexuals.

The Greek Orthodox Archdiocese, in its biennial meeting in 1976 in Philadelphia, "called homosexuality 'an insult to God,' 'blasphemy,' and 'immoral and dangerous perversion,' and 'sinful failure.' "[16]

THE ROMAN CATHOLIC CHURCH

The official Roman Catholic position is very clearly stated in a 1976 Vatican document on sexual ethics, reaffirming condemnation of homosexual acts. However, the Vatican has not ruled on the ordination of avowed homosexuals, and nothing in Canon law specifically prohibits it.

Father John J. McNeill, one of the founders of "Dignity" (an organization for Catholic homosexuals), and a chapter leader in New York City, stated recently that reconsideration of traditional attitudes and approaches to counseling are underway in many religious orders and many dioceses.[17] Father McNeill's opinions were published with the *imprimi potest* of Father General Arrupe in Rome. However, this was recently withdrawn because of its controversial position on the goodness of homosexuality, and Father McNeill has since been asked to limit his activities.

Recently a group of five Roman Catholic theologians wrote a book on sexuality that defended the homosexual lifestyle; it produced considerable consternation within the Roman Catholic hierarchy. Many within the Roman Catholic Church are seeking to find new and more creative ways to minister to persons caught in the sexual maze of homosexuality.

Lutherans are facing similar challenges. And the list goes on and on. . . .

TIME OF DECISION

Is it an overstatement to say the time bomb of gay rights is about to be detonated in the church? I don't believe so. And as the time of decision rapidly approaches, no one can sit on the fence. Each member of these mainline churches needs to become more knowledgeable and personally ready for the impending decisions. Further, Christians need to enter into deliberations in appropriate constitutional ways designated by their church polity to help make these decisions. If not, decisions will be made for them.

During the time the Presbyterian task force met, one young person offered her participation in the decision by writing:

Dear Sirs:

I understand that you are considering the ordination of professing homosexuals. Please would you consider my testimony before deciding.

I grew up in the United Presbyterian Church. It was there that I came to know and to love the Lord Jesus Christ. At age 12 I asked God to fill me with His Holy Spirit. I am sure that He did. Still, while in college I was drawn into a relationship with another woman. I felt great about it at first; my sexual desires were being met, and I was still very much into fulfilling the desires of the flesh.

It was six years before the Holy Spirit began convicting me, slowly, gently at first, then more and more powerfully until I could live with myself no longer. I went to my minister and confessed the whole thing. Breaking off the relationship was a mutual thing fortunately. Both of us continue to run into each other. The Lord gave me a Scripture at the time. It was Revelation 21:5, "Behold I make all things new." He continues to renew our lives daily, and therefore I recognize in this other person a "new creature in Christ Jesus." Praise God! I cannot thank Him enough for lifting me out of the mire and setting me once again on solid ground.

Homosexuality is a dead end. While I was so busy gratifying the desires of my flesh it was impossible for God to give me the desires of my heart. Now He is free to do so. I have dated several young men in the past year, and have enjoyed each date. There has been fellowship and sharing about the Lord Jesus Christ. In addition I have a joy I could not experience before. I can once again look forward to getting married.

God wants the best for us. Let's not settle for second best. God bless you in your decision.

Sincerely in Christ,

I am not giving my name because of my family. (Please understand.)

It is very important that the pressure of decisions and reaction to power politics within the church not heighten our homophobia (fear, hatred, and contempt for homosexuals). We need to respond to the gay crisis responsibly and firmly, but in love.

There is growing resistance within the church to capitulate to the onslaught of gay activism. And there is growing openness on the part of many—hopefully most—to give serious consideration to the meaning of homosexuality and to the ways of ministry that could be redemptive.

3

Our Valley of Decision

HOW WOULD YOU personally respond to your church's changing its stance so that it says a homosexual lifestyle is valid? How would that affect your relationship to your congregation and your denomination? What would this do in terms of your sacrificial giving for the work of the church and your desire to serve on its boards? Are you open to having a homosexual as your pastor?

How would ordaining an avowed, practicing homosexual affect your confidence in the church's leadership and your desire to rear your children in your denomination? How do you believe your spouse would respond to such a decision? Your close friends?

These are difficult questions, but ones that every person seeking to face this issue responsibly must answer.

The gay crisis is not "out there" in a vacuum. It is at our doorstep. The electronic and print media bombard us constantly with new developments. And instead of our witnessing to the culture, we have let the culture witness to us.

The crisis is primarily one of *theology*. But it is also a crisis of *relationship* in the church and in the life of the local congregation. It has to do with the ongoing health of established friendships, and it relates deeply to our unity in Christ.

A THEOLOGICAL CRISIS

Theologically, we are being asked to reinterpret the *content* of Scripture and to change our *approach* to Scripture. Some religious homosexuals have developed for themselves a systematic theology—even an apologetic— to attempt to biblically defend their position; it is popularly called *gay theology*. Gay theology calls for a total change in understanding of biblical texts that address homosexuality and for a redefinition of basic theological concepts concerning:

sexuality and the family;
the holiness of God and His judgment on sin;
the role of God's law for Christians who know God by grace;
the relationship between justification and sanctification;
the biblical meaning of *love*.

This debate has shown that some within the church don't have much biblical theology at all when it comes to *believing*. We have often falsely presumed that because we say the Bible is authoritative and because we ascribe to the creeds, we are firmly accepting the truth set forth in those documents. But we are finding in reality that, though we have drawn near with our lips, our hearts are far from Him.

Great value can come out of theological crises if Christian people take time to study the Scriptures and to speak the truth in love, making their convictions known within the life of the church. God's people cannot afford to flinch from facing difficult issues. Historically, the church has spoken its mind most clearly when forced to do so by theological or moral controversy.

This is just such a time for us; it provides a wonderful opportunity for theological and biblical study, and for spiritual renewal—if we will pay the price for serious inquiry.

In the preface to his outstanding book—*Homosexuality, the Bible, and the Church*—Don Williams writes: "A monumental crisis is upon the church. Avowed and practicing homosexuals demand the sanction of their lifestyles and ordination into the professional clergy. I call this a crisis because it promises to disrupt congregations, shatter church structures, throw confusion into time-honored biblical interpretation, change the social structure of our country, and revoke our fundamental view of Man as male and female."[1]

A RELATIONAL CRISIS

The crisis is not only theological, it's relational—involving ecclesiastical and congregational life. When the United Presbyterian Task Force report came out in favor of ordaining homosexuals, and a minority report was issued in opposition to such ordination, all manner of confusion broke loose in my denomination.

One godly elder, puzzled by so many different voices and different points of view, said with some frustration and anger, "How is it possible that Christians could disagree about what the Bible teaches about homosexuality? How is it possible that even ministers and some theologians could speak in favor of homosexuality as a valid Christian lifestyle? How can we as a denomination be debating as to whether or not a practicing homosexual can be ordained?"

Out of the shock of those days, I wrote my congregation a pastoral letter: ". . . (staff and session) believe the Scriptures are clear about the sinfulness of homosexual acts. . . . We believe it is time to stand up and be counted and to help lead our United Presbyterian Church to take a strong stand to help influence other mainline denominations to do the same. This problem in our country is not going to roll over and die or go away. It must be faced head on. . . ."[2]

TWO POSSIBLE RESPONSES

If the church were to accept the majority report, I believe there would be two different basic reactions within the church. For some, such a decision would prompt a deep heartfelt gratitude that the compassion of the church for broken people was being shown in a greater way. Gay people have been mistreated and insensitively ostracized by the church as modern-day lepers. Some people would feel a decision to receive gay people would be a courageous stand. For them and for practicing homosexuals it would mean new hope for the church. It would mean homosexuals could come "out of the closet" and maybe hold their heads high for the first time. It would help them face their feelings of guilt. But the percentage of people in our denomination who would be pleased and encouraged with this new hope would be very small—I would guess five to fifteen percent. And even some of these would develop apprehensions.

The second group would be discouraged and dismayed by an acceptance of the majority report. They would be confused, frustrated, and angry, and would have feelings of betrayal. Many feel that way already. "How could it have come this far?" they are asking.

Many would find themselves in an untenable position, feeling that their church was defending an immoral way of life, one totally contrary to Scripture. They would ask, "Why did our leadership betray us? Why weren't they committed to our confessional heritage? Why weren't they more sensitive to *our* convictions and feelings as laity when this whole matter was being discussed?" They would sense a definite lack of support from the church in their own lives and families.

Even more basically, people would ask, "Are we still a church when we cease to follow the Lord?" In their hearts many Christians believe homosexual acts are sinful and not consistent with the life and teachings of Christ.

They know that God loves sinners, and because of that love He has sent His Son Jesus to be ". . . the expiation for our sins, and not for ours only but also for the sins of the whole world" (1 John 2:2). They believe that God loves practicing homosexuals—just like He loves each of us whose besetting sin may be pride, selfishness, impatience, gluttony, greed, or even hatred of the homosexual himself. Christ died for *all* of us. Thus, they invite all persons whose besetting sin is homosexual practice to join the rest of them at the foot of the cross in repentance, to know God's forgiveness, and to know the resurrection power of Christ to heal and liberate them from slavery to *that* sin.

They believe that receiving practicing homosexuals into the church, without repentance, would be the same as saying that Jesus Christ justifies sin rather than the sinner. They fear this action would bind homosexuals to live a life of slavery rather than free them to be new persons in Christ, delivered from their sin. They would believe that their church had lost its very soul.

In which of these two groups do you find yourself? Would you be pleased if your denomination was the first to officially endorse the validity of homosexual practice?

Is the movement to change the church's view of homosexual practice as sin and to ordain gay people to the gospel ministry a work of God or an error of man? This is the question we must answer.

II.

A Time to Learn

4

The Real Crisis—
God's Rights

AN OPEN LETTER TO PASTORS

THIS CHAPTER TITLE does not infer that I believe the homosexual crisis is not a real crisis. It is. But the issue before us, at the bottom line, is not *gay* rights, but *God's* rights. We are to seek His will and not our own. God's rights—especially His authority and man's account-ability—are at stake here.

THE LOGIC OF DIVINE AUTHORITY

God is God. As Creator of heaven and earth, He has ultimate authority over His creation. While man is the "crown" of God's creation, he is still the creature and under the Creator's authority.

Jesus Christ, God's Son, "is the image of the invisible God . . . all things were created through him and for him. . . . He is the head of the body, the church; he is the beginning, the first-born from the dead, that in everything he might be pre-eminent. For in him all the fulness of God was pleased to dwell, and through him to reconcile to himself all things, whether on earth or in heaven, making peace by the blood of his cross" (1 Col. 1:15,16,18–20).

And concerning the Son, the day is coming ". . . when he delivers the kingdom to God the Father after destroying every rule and every authority and power" (1 Cor. 15:24).

But until that day, Jesus' provision in the earthly authority structure was first to the apostles, and through them He added the inspired New Testament to the Old Testament; then to leaders whom He raised up within the church throughout the ages (the shepherds of the flock); and finally to the body of Christ at large.

God the Father never *abdicated* His authority to Jesus; nor Jesus to the leadership of the church; nor the shepherds and elders to the sheep. God the Son clearly understood His accountability to His Father; in like manner, the shepherds are accountable to the Chief Shepherd; the flock is accountable to the under-shepherds.

THE REAL CRISIS: GOD'S RIGHTS

God's rights as Creator and Redeemer are infinitely higher than our human rights. He is the one who initiated His relationship with man. It is His world and His church. Only because of His sovereign grace are we His people. Our "rights" must, therefore, yield to His.

God has established the channels through which He exercises His authority within the church. Those channels of authority in the New Covenant are the Lord Jesus Christ, the living Word; Holy Scripture, the written Word; and His appointed leaders in the church who are called to be obedient to Jesus Christ under the authority of Scripture through the leadership of His Spirit.

God's rights are communicated to us under the lordship of Jesus Christ through the Holy Spirit. When He speaks, we listen! Our rights blossom as we bow to His authority within the church. Not to do so is sheer futility and folly as well as anarchy against our Monarch. He is the King who said, "Not every one who says to me, 'Lord, Lord,' shall enter the kingdom of heaven, but he who does the will of my Father who is in heaven" (Matt. 7:21).

The *Magna Carta* of God's authority in the church is Holy Scripture. In Scripture He has made Himself known by His gospel of grace and has revealed His will for our lives. He continues to make His will known by the Holy Spirit speaking in Scripture, which is inspired and authoritative for all God's people.

The human channel through which God has chosen to exercise His authority is His appointed leaders. In virtually every Christian church, leaders are committed by their vows to being led by Scripture and by the Holy Spirit. In the United Presbyterian Church every ordained pastor and elder promises before God and their congregation to "obey Jesus Christ under the authority of Scripture."[1]

GOD'S RIGHTS AND WE SHEPHERDS

I sense the weight of responsibility upon my shoulders in being a pastor and in caring for the flock over which the Lord has appointed me. I am mindful that we Presbyterian pastors carry this heavy responsibility in the homosexual debate because our polity places that responsibility clearly with us and with our elders. We are responsible before God in our stewardship of leadership. He will hold us accountable and so will our flocks.

Listen to the writer of Hebrews: "Obey your leaders and submit to them; for they are keeping watch over your souls, as men who will have to give account. Let them do this joyfully, and not sadly, for that would be of no advantage to you" (Heb. 13:17).

Paul said to the Ephesians that ours is a divinely appointed office by which "to equip the saints for the work of the ministry, for building up the body of Christ" (Eph. 4:12). Peter tells us that we, as fellow elders, are to tend the flock of God willingly, not by domineering but by example, clothed with humility toward God and one another (see 1 Pet. 5:2–5).

Paul warned the elders at Ephesus, "Take heed to yourselves and to all the flock, in which the Holy Spirit has made you overseers, to care for the Church of God which he obtained with the blood of His own Son" (Acts 20:28).

THE PATTERN FOR SHEPHERDS

Jesus set the pattern personally for all pastors and elders. He was the Good Shepherd who laid down His life for the sheep. He was not a hireling; His safety did not matter. He had counted the cost. In fact, the Shepherd Himself became the Lamb! The Good Shepherd who had power "to lay down His life and power to take it again" did not use that power for Himself, but used that power totally for the well-being of the sheep. Here was One who knew and loved His sheep so personally that He left the ninety and nine and searched for the one who was lost (see John 10; Matt. 18:12,13).

But note well the contrast between the Good Shepherd and those shepherds described by the ancient prophet Ezekiel.

> The weak you have not strengthened, the sick you have not healed, the crippled you have not bound up, the strayed you have not brought back, the lost you have not sought, and with force and harshness you have ruled them. So they were scattered, because there was no shepherd; and they became food for all the wild beasts. My sheep were scattered, they wandered over all the mountains and on every high hill; my sheep were scattered over all the face of the earth, with none to search or seek for them (Ezek. 34:4–6).

40

God's response was judgment. "Thus says the Lord God, Behold, I am against the shepherds . . . " (Ezek. 34:10).

I want to remind all of us as pastors that we are called to bring back the straying sheep. *We are not called to wink at sin. We are not called to say the straying sheep are "okay" in their wandering and ordain their wandering ways as viable alternative lifestyles.*

The Head of our church does call His shepherds and people to *public morality*—that is, to a ministry of compassion for people, to a respect for human rights, and to advocacy of social justice. He loves the weak, the broken, the oppressed, and the person in need.

But Jesus also calls us to *private morality.* Our words and our attitudes are important. He emphasized God's intention of fidelity. What Jesus thought about marriage and sexuality is of great importance for our study.

Jesus Christ was not soft on sexual sin as some want to say. He was a lover of sinners and treated them sensitively, even those whom He confronted strongly and directly. But as He forgave them, He then said, "Go, and sin no more" (John 8:11, KJV). There is no evidence that Jesus' forgiveness ever left people in their sin. Instead, it led them to hate their sin and turn from it.

Jesus never spoke specifically to the issue of homosexuality. He didn't need to. The Old Testament was extremely clear on the subject, and the problem was not widespread in Israel because of that Old Testament teaching. But this is not to say that Jesus did not speak clearly about sexual morality. He spoke clearly and powerfully.

But what comes out of the mouth proceeds from the heart, and this defiles a man. For out of the heart come evil thoughts, murder, adultery, fornication, theft, false witness, slander. These are what defile a man . . . (Matt. 15:18–20).

41

THE SAGA OF THE REVEREND LUKE WARM

The church has not been taking Jesus seriously. Why not? For God's sake, why not? Because we are *gutless*. We are influenced by the numbers game. "But everybody's doing it."

Since when did numbers determine morality? This is why we face the present crisis with homosexuality: Both the people and their leaders in the church are committing adultery with impunity. Do we respond? No, we're afraid we'll make some waves.

For example, when one of our leading clergy in the West divorced his wife and married another woman in his church, the incident was never discussed at the presbytery level. The man was "kicked upstairs" to an administrative job in the denomination without any evidence of confrontation or repentance.

The same thing was true of another minister in the South whose wife passed away. He married another woman soon after her death and then divorced *her*. A short time later he was promoted to an administrative position in another presbytery. God help us! Why doesn't somebody speak out?

A dear friend from seminary, a pastor in another part of the country, is divorcing his wife to marry his secretary, leaving his five children behind. I met his brother, who is also a pastor and another friend of past years, at the General Assembly in Baltimore, only to have him sheepishly introduce me to *his* new (second) wife. That same day I heard that one of our national administrative staff members couldn't be at the Assembly because he was on an around-the-world trip with his new wife. I wanted to weep! Or shout! Or something!

You who are the shepherds, how do you deal with this? How do you respond to the lordship of Christ in these matters and with our vow in ordination to obey Him? Are we not accountable to Him? And are we not accountable to Him to hold one another accountable?

Brethren, we have caved in to the culture. It has tamed us. We have lost heart. Or else we have neither courage nor integrity. We have come to fear man more than God.

You and I are not authorities unto ourselves. We are under authority—the authority of God and His constituted leaders in the church. His honor is at stake through us. We are His ordained leadership. We did not choose Him, for Christ declared, ". . . I chose you and appointed you that you should go and bear fruit and that your fruit should abide . . ." (John 15:16).

Do we yield to Him and follow His authority in our personal lives? How about in our view of marriage and human sexuality? Is Jesus Christ Lord over how we seek to understand and minister to practicing homosexuals? The church is at a crossroads and we, as pastors, are out in the intersection. We must answer these questions personally—for ourselves. But we must do much more.

Are we ready *as a church* to answer these same questions about God's rights? Do we care about the wholesale breakdown and disintegration of the family in our society and in the church?

Allow me to suggest an answer. I believe we have lost sight of the importance of family life and the importance of marital fidelity because, in large measure, we have bought the lie that "there is nothing I can do about it." As I stated a moment ago, many of our own warriors—our ordained leaders—are involved in marriage failures and in moral failures and therefore do not have the heart, nor the armor, to fight that battle. We are embarrassed even to talk about it. We don't want it on the agenda—and if it gets on, it "smacks of legalism." A conspiracy of silence has developed.

It is tragic but true that men rot from within. Brethren, we *can* resist our temptations. It is not okay to divorce our wives. It is not okay to run around with another woman inside or outside of our churches. It is not okay to marry that other woman who has stolen heart and body away, and to break up another home. It's a cop-out to go to another place and start life over again with a new position. It is dishonest to graduate into the hierarchy, living out our ordination vows only at a cosmetic level.

Allow me the privilege of sharing my own struggles. There have been times during my ministry when I recognized the beginning of my emotional involvement with a woman. I have found it necessary to deal with those situations with radical surgery at the very beginning stages. The sooner I dealt with it, the easier it was. I found that I could never allow my mind to linger on the person or on the feelings. Otherwise, those feelings would begin to grow, and dealing with them would become very difficult.

The most difficult time occurred in a former parish when I had worked closely with a person in youth ministry. We spent considerable time together planning and leading meetings. Everything was above board except that emotional ties deepened through companionship and our common ministry with young people. My thoughts began to linger upon that person, although I continually rebuked and resisted them with a good measure of success.

Then I received a Christmas note from her expressing her respect and love for me. She was not intending something significant by her words, but because of my vulnerability the note revealed to me feelings that were not healthy and could become dangerous. I acted immediately, telling her that I felt her words were inappropriate and that the response within me was even more inappropriate. I gave the note back to her and asked her to share it with her husband so they could talk things out from their end. I then went to two fellow pastors in the presbytery and told them of my own vulnerability and determination to honor God and my wife and family in my relationships with all other women.

I told them I needed their support and I asked them to hold me accountable. And they have. God very quickly removed those feelings and restored them to a proper respectful distance.

As pastors we are unusually vulnerable because of our compassion and because of the needs so many women share with us. Therefore, we must be extra careful and keep a healthy distance. We must determine ahead of time that our response in such situations will be based on the teaching of Scripture and not on our emotional reaction of the moment.

One of my close friends in the ministry fell in love with a young woman in his youth group. They had spent countless hours together planning youth meetings and outings. They counseled together, listened to one another's struggles, and became emotionally involved. But it didn't stop there. This "loving and sensitive" relationship led to the desire to fulfill one another's needs more deeply. They became physically involved.

I heard of his plan to divorce his precious wife, whom I had shared in leading to Christ fifteen years before, and I asked to see him. We spent hours together looking at Scripture and talking about his ministry and his vows. He had already left his church and was selling cars. He was ready to give up the ministry, at least for a time, until he could get things worked out with the presbytery.

His wife was near an emotional breakdown. The children's school work revealed their emotional suffering. His parents were crushed. The congregation he had served for years was in shambles. His own life was in a constant turmoil. God's will was obvious to him. But God's will was no longer primary.

God's rights didn't matter. God's people and their sufferings were unimportant. God's truth was irrelevant. The

45

suffering of his family could be pushed aside. The broken lives of the kids in that youth group couldn't touch him. Nothing made a difference.

What mattered were *his* desires, *his* willfulness, *his* lust. He wanted out of his responsibility so he could run away and find freedom from his family and from his mother's dominance since childhood. And in the process, it was "so long" to God, the Bible, the church, and his family.

You know, that's the story of the Garden (see Gen. 3:1–19). And because of sin, it's the story of all of us until God's grace touches us and our hearts, and we then turn and receive God's amazing grace. We say yes to Jesus, yes to His cross, yes to the Resurrection, and yes to Christ as *Lord.*

THE BOTTOM LINE

Pastors, the issue before us is not homosexuality. It is morality. The issue before us is not the ordination of homosexuals—gay rights. The issue before us is God's rights—God's rights to call us to Himself, to call us to live as His obedient children, to call us to be holy (because He is holy), to call us to moral purity and integrity.

What if your wife were paralyzed early in your married life? Are you still called to be faithful to her? Yes, yes, yes, a thousand times yes. Sex is not God. Relationships are blessed by physical love but not totally dependent upon it.

He has not said we would not suffer. In fact, He has promised that if we follow Christ and deny self, we *will* suffer. There *will* be a cross. The cross is central to Christian discipleship. Jesus told us that at the beginning of our Christian life.

Do you mean that if I no longer love my wife and I've found someone who complements my life much more fully, that I should reject my desires and go ahead and live with my wife? That is what God says. He is able to make all things new (see Rev. 21:5) and that includes giving you a new love for your wife. And He is able to give her a new love for you.

Your marriage is not hopeless. Your wedding vows were not made on the basis of feelings but on the basis of the will. They were written with that in mind. The church knew that you and I couldn't operate on the basis of feelings. It had to be on the basis of a commitment of the will, a binding agreement not only between two people, but also among those persons, the church, and God.

Let's face it, at the pastoral level we have been intimidated; we do not want to appear holier-than-thou, self-righteous, or judgmental. We have deified tolerance. We have made church discipline our ultimate heresy. Because of abuses of the past and a pluralistic church, we have lost our ability to stand against personal sin with the same clarity and the same passion with which we have stood against social sin.

Further, most of us have adopted the "Lone Ranger" model of churchmanship: Keep your own house clean if you can, but if you can't, keep quiet about it and you won't rock the boat. With any luck, neither will anyone else.

Another breakdown in righteousness comes because we are not close enough to fellow pastors to really love each other. If we don't know each other and love each other, then we can't share our struggles and our failings with one another. When we are not a supportive fellowship—not bearing one another's burdens—it's very difficult for one of us who is struggling in a marriage to reach out for help. We are left to work it out alone. And we don't.

Brothers and sisters, let us call one another to love and good deeds. God calls us to moral integrity and courage. It is time for judgment to begin once more at the house of

God. It is time God had His way again among His shepherds. Our people want things to be in proper order—they are crying out to be heard and helped.

Let us covenant together to be the persons of God we vowed we would be.

5

Text and Context

THERE IS CONSIDERABLE confusion in our society and in the church concerning homosexuality and homosexual practice. People are asking for a clear word rather than a muffled sound. They are asking for a biblical word, a word from the Lord, rather than the changing opinions of men. They want both firmness and compassion, which reflect the character of our Lord when confronting moral laxity and broken people.

I am mindful that a Scripture text out of context often becomes a pretext. However, a text in context and interpreted within the total perspective of Scripture becomes God's method of revealing truth.

A good friend of mine (Ben Patterson—a Presbyterian pastor in California who has helped me shape this chapter) tells the story of his first encounter with a homosexual in January, 1972. He had spoken at a high school retreat. In the course of conversation following one of the evening meetings, a young man (let's call him Larry) admitted his gayness to Ben. Larry told Ben that God had given him victory over the problem, but he was concerned that he might fall back into his old ways when he went home.

Ben says, "Two weeks after the retreat I received a letter from Larry. It read, in part:

We started back to school today, and since I was back among the multitudes of males, I was back to those good old cravings. . . . You know, Ben, I've thought a lot about Christianity lately, and homosexuality, and I've decided that until I get to a point where I don't think the way I do now, then I'm going to be the way I am now; and frankly, I'm not sure I want to change. The big question: why can't I be both?[1]

Ben goes on to say, "I never answered Larry's letter, or his question. At the time, all I could have done was mumble a few Scriptures in condemnation of his condition and his behavior and tell him I would pray for him. Somehow that just didn't seem to be enough. This feeling of overwhelming inadequacy was combined with a near physical revulsion for his lifestyle. I found myself procrastinating in responding to him until I finally misplaced or 'lost' his address. I confess this to my shame."[2]

Ben is not alone. I have faced similar questions with dozens of men and women struggling to define their own viewpoints on homosexual practice. And I've had the same experience with many pastors who are wrestling with how to guide their people and lead our denomination in the matter.

BIBLICAL UNDERSTANDING OF SEXUALITY

A proper discussion of the theological understanding of homosexuality must begin with the Creation and Fall narratives in Genesis 1:26–31, 2:18–25, and 3:1–24.

The Creation narrative establishes us as persons who possess a specific sexual identity. "So God created man in his own image . . . male and female he created them" (Gen. 1:27). His intention through this differentiation of the sexes was to complete the order of Creation.

The point is this: Sexual differentiation is essential to

understanding what is fully human. Don Williams says it well:

> God does not create Man alone, neither does He create man/man or woman/woman. God creates Man as male and female, and only in community together is the image of God seen upon the earth. Thus the old myths of the androgenous (bisexual or unisexual) man are rejected and all ambiguity in the relationship between the sexes is removed. Man is created for another. That other is woman. Their relationship is ordered by God.[3]

Therefore, to be created in the image of God includes being in relationship as male and female. In Genesis 1 we discover that to be human is to share humanity with the opposite sex.

In Genesis 2 we find this theme of the complementary nature of male and female expanded. The incompleteness of creation is introduced when God says, " '. . . It is not good that the man should be alone; I will make him a helper fit for him' " (2:18). According to Williams, "Thus as God has directly made the man, so he directly makes the woman from man, and in her he receives the helper who makes him a complete person."[4]

The purpose of sexual union is not only for procreation, but for the development of a deeper relationship. In Creation, humanity was "one flesh" because woman was taken from man (Gen. 2:21–23). In sexual intercourse a man and woman become one flesh again as they enter into their physical union.

In Genesis 3 we find the goodness of God's creation distorted by sin and the divine pattern for male–female relationship is marred. Estrangement and alienation replaced God's intention. God's good gift to male and female was distorted through rebellion and pride. Strain between the sexes was the result.

Homosexuality is one result of this disjointedness. To be sure, it is not the only one. Adultery (see Gen. 26:10), incest (see Gen. 19:36), rape (see Gen. 34:2), and prostitution (see Gen. 38:15ff) also pose continual threats to sexual wholeness. It is in the light of the Fall and the damage done to our humanity and sexuality that homosexuality and the other deviations from God's created order must be understood.

OLD TESTAMENT PASSAGES

There are specific Old Testament texts that address clearly the issue of homosexuality. We find in these texts that each of them is supportive of our thesis that God's declarations against homosexuality and other sexual deviations are to protect His purposes in creation for marriage and family life, His purpose in creating Man male and female.

Genesis 18 & 19

First is the story of Sodom and Gomorrah in Genesis 18 and 19. God made a covenant or agreement with Abraham saying, " 'And I will make of you a great nation, and I will bless you . . . and by you all the families of the earth shall bless themselves' " (Gen. 12:2,3). Abraham and his nephew, Lot, decided to part ways. Lot chose to settle in Sodom. "Now the men of Sodom were wicked, great sinners against the Lord" (Gen. 13:13). This observation prepares us for the events of Genesis 18:16–19; 29. Notice the context.

In Chapter 18 we find the Lord and two angels visiting Abraham, telling him of the impending destruction of Sodom. Abraham, out of concern for Lot and the city, pleads for a reprieve if ten righteous people can be found there. And God agrees.

The account given to us in Genesis 19:4–11 is a description of what happened when the two angels visited the city—"crime and punishment." This is the event that confirmed that the city was wicked and deserved total destruction.[5]

In Genesis 19 we find this plot: Lot was the only one who extended hospitality to the angelic visitors when they came to Sodom. Following dinner, the men of the city surrounded the home and called out, " 'Where are the men who came to you tonight? Bring them out to us, that we may know them' " (19:5). Lot pleads with the men, " '. . . do not act so wickedly' " (19:7). Then Lot defends the strong ancient law of hospitality, " ' . . . do nothing to these men, for they have come under the shelter of my roof' " (19:8). In place of the men he offers his daughters " ' . . . who have not *known* man . . . do to them as you please . . .' " (19:8, emphasis mine).

They rejected Lot, the alien sojourner, and served as their own judge. They would not be dissuaded, and they proceeded with their plan when Lot was rescued by the angels. Sodom's sin was here established, and the judgment of God was righteous and swift.

The central question in interpreting the passage is, what were the men of Sodom seeking when they called upon Lot to bring out the men—"that we may know them" (Gen. 19:5)?

Virtual unanimous interpretation of this passage for over twenty centuries has been that the motivation of the men of Sodom was homosexual lust linked with murderous hostility. This overwhelmingly predominant position has been held by John Calvin; Martin Luther; Karl Barth; *The Westminster Study Bible;* the *New English Bible;* Brown, Driver, and Briggs (authors of the *Hebrew Lexicon of the Old Testament*); Gerhard von Rad; Bruce Metzger;

William Everett Harrison; Paul Jewett; and Donald Williams.

However, in 1955, Derrick Bailey, an Anglican, defied the view of two millennia of orthodox consensus and said that "to know" meant to "get acquainted with."[6] Bailey teaches that since Lot was a sojourner he had no right to extend hospitality to these foreigners. The men of Sodom, by their hostility, were sinning against the ancient practice of hospitality. Bailey ultimately concludes that the Sodom story has no reference to homosexual practice at all. John J. McNeill, an avowed homosexual and Roman Catholic priest, is the principal popularizer of Bailey's thoughts through his own book, *The Church and The Homosexual*. But even McNeill acknowledges that Bailey probably overstated the case.[7] David Bartlett of the Chicago Theological Seminary, a supporter of gay theology, disagrees with Bailey directly. "The integrity of the story indicates that what is at issue in each instance is intercourse, and not just getting acquainted."[8]

I should hope so! After all, unless all of modern biology is amiss, Adam went far beyond "getting acquainted" with Eve to populate planet Earth. For the Scripture tells us, Adam *knew* his wife.

However, having pointed out the meaning of the word "know," I want to emphasize that this story does *not* give us the basis for opposition to all homosexual acts as sinful. The clear implication here is that homosexual rape is wrong and in this case probably by heterosexuals, or Lot's offer of his daughters would have made little sense.

On the other hand, the Sodom event is consistent with and assumes the biblical view of Man created male and female. "God's judgment on violent 'unnatural' sexual acts is clear. Sodom and Gomorrah become the picture of total corruption deserving God's righteous judgment throughout."[9]

Leviticus 18:22; 20:13

Known as the "Holiness Code," God's clear command is, " ' . . . You shall be holy; for I the *Lord* your God am holy' " (Lev. 19:2, emphasis mine). The subject is God's call to Israel to be a different people, separated from those who practiced paganism all around them. The text in Leviticus 18:22 reads, " 'You shall not lie with a male as with a woman; it is an abomination.' " This is expanded in Leviticus 20:13, " 'If a man lies with a male as with a woman, both of them have committed an abomination; they shall be put to death, their blood is upon them.' "

The passages listed below are set in the context of God's judgment upon sexual crimes and are an expansion of the Ten Commandments:

> seduction of a virgin (Exod. 22:16ff);
> rape of an unbetrothed virgin (Deut. 22:28ff);
> rape of a betrothed virgin (Deut. 22:23–27);
> adultery with or rape of another's wife (Lev. 20:10; Deut. 22:22);
> incest (Lev. 20:11,12,14; Deut. 27:20,22,23);
> bestiality (Exod. 22:19; Lev. 18:23; 20:15,16);
> homosexuality (Lev. 18:22; 20:13).

If you study these passages you will find God's purpose is to preserve the sanctity of marriage and the home. This is evident from the severe penalty of death He prescribed for the sins of homosexual practice, adultery, incest, and bestiality.

Bartlett comments that these concerns for the society and for the family as treated in Leviticus "are more responsible and more sophisticated than simple prooftexting."[10]

But there is a problem: Why should we take these passages of Leviticus seriously for our day and not the surrounding passages of rituals and dietary laws, such as the law not to eat shrimp, crab, and oysters (Lev. 11) or rare steak (Lev. 17:14)?

It is because of the numerous New Testament passages that pointedly speak to and set aside the *dietary laws* (Matt. 15:10–19; Acts 10:9–16; Rom. 14:1–4, 13–21). Other passages clearly set aside the *ceremonial laws* (Gal. 3:1–14; 5:1–12; Heb. 8–10).

By contrast, the *moral law* of God in the Pentateuch is strongly reaffirmed and even stressed in the New Testament—not as a way of salvation nor as the means for being right with God, but as a revelation of God's unchanging and righteous will for His people to bring us to Christ (Matt. 5:20; Rom. 3:19,20). Gay theologians argue the "all or nothing" principle, but they do not apply it to themselves. To eliminate all of the "Holiness Code" would eliminate God's judgment against bestiality, incest, and child sacrifice—along with adultery and homosexuality. I trust they are not asking us to do that.

We do not use Leviticus 18 and 20 as a binding law upon Christians. The law is meant to bring us to Christ. We do not put those who violate this law to death, even though they deserve death because of their sin. Paul tells us in Romans 6:23 that we all deserve death because of our sins. But Christ has died *for* us. He has paid the proper penalty for us.

We see in the "Holiness Code" another illustration of the *total context* of Scripture—that God made man male and female and intended faithful heterosexual relations within marriage. He hasn't changed His mind.

THE NEW TESTAMENT

The Gospels

"While it is true that Jesus never mentions homosexuality in the Gospels, it is also true that whenever He speaks about human sexuality He presupposes heterosexuality," says Williams.[11] In the Sermon on the Mount, Jesus strengthened the force of the Law. He taught it was not enough to merely refrain from the act of adultery. " ' . . . every one who looks at a woman lustfully has already committed adultery with her in his heart' " (Matt. 5:28).

This point is made even stronger when you consider how Jesus argued the meaning of Moses' bill of divorce. The appeal He made was not to the law but to creation. " ' . . . Have you not read that he who made them from the beginning made them male and female, and said, "For this reason a man shall leave his father and mother and be joined to his wife, and the two shall become one"? So they are no longer two but one. What therefore God has joined together, let no man put asunder' " (Matt. 19:4–6). Here we have Jesus emphasizing the Creation account—man as male and female—as the basis for marriage. We see Him saying that in marriage the two become one flesh, and that God is the source of this union. We also see that Jesus' view of God's intention is a marriage relationship that lasts. Thus we see *why* Jesus took adultery and the lustful eye so seriously.

Jesus' only alternative to marriage is celibacy, becoming a eunuch for the sake of God's kingdom (see Matt. 19:10–12). Throughout the four Gospels He *never* entertained the option of homosexuality. In Jesus Christ is the total affirmation: Sexuality is male and female.

PAULINE EPISTLES

Romans 1:26,27

The Book of Romans, the pinnacle of Paul's doctrine, begins with the reality of God's righteousness (1:17). The further context of the book speaks of God's wrath, His holiness, our sin, new standing in Christ, and life in the Holy Spirit—in the church and in the world.

In the context of God's wrath over man's sin, we find Romans 1:26 and 27:

... God gave them up to dishonorable passions. Their women exchanged natural relations for unnatural, and the men likewise gave up natural relations with women and were consumed with passion for one another, men committing shameless acts with men and receiving in their own persons the due penalty for their error.

This is the most devastating passage in the Bible for practicing homosexuals. Paul gives a theological rationale for condemning homosexual behavior. God's judgment gives persons freedom to go their own way. "God gives them up" to do what they want. Homosexual lust and activity are denounced as "dishonorable passions," which abandon "natural relations."

The Greek phrase, *fusike chresis,* which is translated "natural relations," is a direct reference to God's created order, with nature (Greek, *fusis*) being used here and in other places in Romans to describe what God intends to be the way male and female should relate sexually.

Paul's condemnation of the sin of homosexuality becomes even more pointed when it is seen in the context of his preceding remarks in Romans 1:18–25. The apostle traces the whole range of human brokenness and sin back to the primal disorder of idolatry. Man's root sin is his refusal to acknowledge his "creatureliness," worshiping the creation rather than the Creator. This cataclysmic fracture in his relationship to God leads inevitably to a broken personal identity of which homosexuality is a prime, glaring example. Disorder in communion with God leads to disorder in all relationships, including our sexuality.

"Paul's implicit point is that both idolatry and certain sexual practices change the created order. According to the created order, males are supposed to worship God and to have intercourse with women. Women are supposed to worship God and have intercourse with men. When people violate the order by worshiping creatures, the punishment they receive is a further violation of the created order; they have intercourse with members of the same sex."[12]

The significance of the above statement by Bartlett is intensified when you realize that he leans *toward* ordination of homosexuals! That inclination, however, has not altered his careful perception of biblical interpretation.

Some homosexual apologists, such as Bailey and McNeill, have tried to sidestep this passage by asserting that Paul was castigating homosexual lust and promiscuity rather than homosexual acts. They also suggest that when Paul talked about "natural relations," he was referring to the individual person's natural affectional preference. Thus, in their view, if a homosexual was to do what is "natural" for *him*, he must love a person of the same sex. To do otherwise would be for him *unnatural*.

Romans and Greeks had long rationalized homosexuality, and even Plato in the *Symposium* gave it his approval. It is unthinkable that Paul would not designate which kinds of homosexual behavior he would approve, especially given the place it occupies in his thesis regarding the fall of man in the first chapter of Romans. He certainly drew distinctions when it came to other ethical questions. He drew lines between sufficient and insufficient grounds for divorce. He differentiated between a proper and an improper use of meat offered to idols. He contrasted constructive exhortation with judgmental rebuke. He discriminated between good and bad use of the law.

But here, with this major issue, Paul made no distinctions. Both homosexual lust *and* behavior were categorically rejected and condemned as sinful. The *acts* were condemned.

59

1 Corinthians 6:9,10

The apostle took the same approach in 1 Corinthians 6:9. Here he used two Greek words to refer to homosexuals: *malakio* and *arsenokoitai*. The first most likely designates the passive or "female" partner in homosexual liaison; the latter refers perhaps to the active or "male" partner. But in any event, the emphasis is upon the *act*, not the intention. John M. Batteau points out that these words were used consistently by Greek authors to apply to the full spectrum of homosexuality, both promiscuous and monogamous.[13] Only the wildest of religious speculation can avoid the conclusion that Paul knew exactly what he meant and how he would be understood when he used these terms to say, ". . . Do not be deceived; neither the immoral, nor idolators, nor adulterers, nor homosexuals . . . will inherit the kingdom of God" (1 Cor. 6:9, 10). And Paul went on to say, "And such were some of you . . ." (6:11). The good news of grace in Romans is also true in 1 Corinthians 6. ". . . But you were washed, you were sanctified, you were justified in the name of the Lord Jesus Christ and in the Spirit of our God" (6:11). Paul never stopped at the point of judgment. He moved to the beauty of forgiven sin.

1 Timothy 1:8–10

Paul began in 1 Timothy 1:8 to repeat his theme from Romans that the law is good if it is used to help us know (a) the depth of our sin, and (b) God's grace to forgive the repentant through Christ. He said the law is for ". . . the lawless and disobedient, for the ungodly and sinners, for the unholy and profane . . ." (1:9). And then (v. 10) he wrote "immoral persons, sodomites, kidnapers, liars, perjurers, and whatever else is contrary to sound doctrine." The active partner in a homosexual relationship (*arsenokoitai*) is translated "sodomite." Again, as in Leviticus,

Romans, and 1 Corinthians, the practicing homosexual is in bad company. But, as before, he is promised grace and forgiveness upon turning to Christ.

IN SUMMARY

From Genesis to Leviticus, from Romans and 1 Corinthians to 1 Timothy, the message is consistently the same: God created Man as male and female. Our sexuality is to be fulfilled in faithful heterosexual relationships within marriage. God does not alter His message to fit the culture. It is the same in every culture. He calls His people to live in contrast to the culture.

Everywhere in Scripture He condemns the *objective behavior*, not just the motives or subjective feelings. Everywhere He seeks to fulfill His original, pre-Fall purposes for marriage and family in the fabric of society. He constantly calls His people to be holy, "For I the Lord am holy."

It's the text in context.

6

Fathers Know Best

"**N**O PHRASE WITHIN the Constitution can be construed explicitly to prohibit the ordination of self-affirming (avowed) practicing homosexual Christians."[1] It is this one sentence from the task force's majority report that is at issue in the future stance of the United Presbyterian Church on the homosexual crisis.

In the last chapter, we dealt directly with the Scriptures in addressing this question. In this chapter, let us turn our attention briefly to those who have helped build on the apostolic foundations—the Fathers of the church, both ancient and modern—who are in clear agreement as to the role and authority of Scripture in making moral decisions. That their agreement *is* clear is crucial, because if the Scriptures can be reinterpreted to call the homosexual lifestyle valid for Christians, then there is no way to assure the validity and stability of *anything* we believe, either in doctrine or practice. We will be in danger of approaching theology like cut flowers, looking only at their present state and forgetting the rich roots and the fertile soil that made growth possible in the first place.

Sometimes we get the feeling that the homosexual issue is a new one, unique to the late twentieth century. This problem is not new. As I mentioned earlier, it was prominent in both the ancient Greek and Roman cultures. So, let us hear our Fathers on the subject.

THE EARLY CHURCH

The apocryphal writings of the early centuries—Testaments of the Twelve Patriarchs (Test. Naph. 3:4,5; Test. Benj. 9:1), and the Second Book of Enoch (2 Enoch 10:4), give a homosexual interpretation of the sin of Sodom. The historian Josephus (A.D. 37–96) made the same implication in his writings (Antiquities, I, 11,3). There was broad, indeed universal, consensus among these ancient writers that homosexuality was sin.

Much of early church philosophy about marriage came from Augustine, the beloved fifth-century bishop who believed that one of its "greatest goods" was the product, children. He was firm in his denunciation of homosexuality:

> These shameful acts against nature, such as were committed in Sodom, ought everywhere and always to be detested and punished. If all nations were to do such things, they would (equally) be held guilty of the same crime by the law of God, which has not so made men that they should use one another in this way.[2]

Thomas Aquinas, writing in the thirteenth century, classified sexual sins as those against chastity and those against nature. He called homosexuality a sin against both.

In these later centuries, sexuality was often dealt with in relation to the criterion of procreation. Sins "contrary to nature" that violated the procreative purpose were considered more radical than others.

THE MATTER OF "NEW LIGHT"

The Presbyterian Task Force questions whether the Holy Spirit may not now be leading the church into new truth which it could not have received before.

Drawing attention to the words of Jesus concerning the Holy Spirit—

> I have yet many things to say to you, but you cannot bear them now. When the Spirit of truth comes, He will guide you into all the truth; for He will not speak on His own authority, but whatever He hears He will speak, and He will declare to you the things that are to come (John 16:12,13)

—some say it is consistent with Scripture that God's will may undergo change. Others say "new truth" is in conflict with what the Scriptures and our Confessions have taught in the past.

I believe that to endorse homosexuality as a valid Christian lifestyle would be "new light" *not from* the Scripture, but *in conflict with* Scripture. "If then the light in you is darkness, how great is the darkness!" (Matt. 6:23). But homosexual proponents come to the Scripture stating that the assumption of our forefathers was that God "hath more light yet to break out of his Holy Word."

Thus, the following was incorporated into the original mandate of the General Assembly in 1976:

> Because God continues to reveal more of himself and his will in each succeeding age, we do not believe that a position taken in any one period sets forth the final understanding of his Word to the Church. We know that there is always more light to break forth from the Bible through the work of the Holy Spirit. Jesus said, "I have many things to say to you, but you cannot bear them now. When the Spirit of Truth comes, he will guide you into all the truth."[3]

OUR CONFESSIONAL HERITAGE

It was not the intention of our forefathers, nor of the General Assembly, that the new light coming from the Holy Spirit would be contradictory to Scripture. For the

Puritan forefathers it was new light "to break *out of* his Holy Word." It was new insight, new illumination, new perspective *out of* Scripture, not *apart* from Scripture.

This stance is consistent with our *Book of Confessions.* In the Confession of 1967 we read:

> The one sufficient revelation of God is Jesus Christ, the Word of God incarnate, to whom the Holy Spirit bears unique and authoritative witness through the Holy Scriptures, *which are received and obeyed as the word of God written. . . .* The church has received the books of the Old and New Testaments as prophetic and apostolic testimony *IN which it hears the word of God and BY which its faith and obedience are nourished . . . .*
>
> As God has spoken his word in diverse cultural situations, the church is *confident that he will continue to speak THROUGH the Scriptures* in a changing world and in every form of human culture (emphasis mine).[4]

Here the emphasis is upon the Holy Spirit and the Word written—not the Spirit apart from Scripture and not Scripture apart from the Spirit. Both point us to Jesus Christ, the living Word, as central. The Scripture is that "in which" and "by which" the church hears the Word of God and grows in faith and obedience. Because God has spoken in a variety of cultural situations and places, "the church is confident that He will continue to speak *through* the Scriptures."

In 1967 we reaffirmed our Reformed conviction that God speaks *in, by,* and *through* the Scriptures. But within the United Presbyterian Church our confessional stance is not limited to the Confession of 1967. In our Book of Confessions, adopted in 1967 as part of our Constitution, we include many outstanding Reformed statements of faith.

The Declaration of Barmen is such a statement. It came

from the German Evangelical Church when they confessed their faith and their opposition to Hitler and his
misuse of the church. It concludes its introduction with
these words:

> If you find that we are speaking contrary to Scripture, then
> do not listen to us! But if you find that we are taking our
> stand upon Scripture, then let no fear or temptation keep
> you from treading with us the path of faith and obedience to
> the Word of God, in order that God's people be of one mind
> upon earth and that we in faith experience what he himself
> has said: "I will never leave you nor forsake you." There-
> fore, "Fear not, little flock, for it is your Father's good plea-
> sure to give you the kingdom."[5]

THE WESTMINSTER CONFESSION

Our confession of faith in the United Presbyterian
Church of the United States of America before 1967 was
the Westminster Confession of Faith. It is the Confession
under which most of us in the ministry today were ordained. Its statement relative to Scripture is also strong.

> The authority of the Holy Scripture, for which it ought to be
> believed and obeyed, dependeth not upon the testimony of
> any man or church, but wholly upon God (who is truth
> itself), the author thereof; and therefore it is to be received
> because it is the Word of God.[6]

> The whole counsel of God, concerning all things necessary
> for his own glory, man's salvation, faith, and life, is either
> expressly set down in Scripture, or by good and necessary
> consequence may be deduced from Scripture; unto which
> nothing at any time is to be added, whether by new revela-
> tions of the Spirit or traditions of men. Nevertheless we
> acknowledge the inward illumination of the Spirit of God to
> be necessary for the saving understanding of such things as
> are revealed in the Word. . . .[7]

These passages speak both to the authority of Scripture and to the importance and necessity of the Holy Spirit's enabling faith and understanding. They also underscore that no *"new revelations of the Spirit"* or of *"the traditions of men"* are to be added to our faith that are *contrary* to Scripture. New light? Yes, but from Scripture.

One other sentence from the Confession describes the principle of interpretation.

> The infallible rule of interpretation of Scripture is the Scripture itself; and therefore, when there is a question about the true and full sense of any Scripture (which is not manifold, but one), it may be searched and known by other places that speak more clearly.[8]

This becomes particularly important when we seek to understand the interrelatedness of passages dealing with sexuality and homosexuality.

THE "SWISS" CONFESSION

The Second Helvetic (Swiss) Confession is also an important part of our *Book of Confessions*. Dr. Edward A. Dowey, Jr., of Princeton Seminary, describes it this way: "The highest authority among Reformed confessions has generally been granted to the Second Helvetic (Swiss) Confession."[9]

The first chapter begins with the place of Scripture.

> We believe and confess the canonical Scriptures of the holy prophets and apostles of both Testaments to be the true Word of God, and to have sufficient authority of themselves, not of men. For God himself spoke to the fathers, prophets, apostles, and still speaks to us *through* the Holy Scriptures.

> And *in* this Holy Scripture, the universal Church of Christ has the most complete exposition of all that pertains to a saving faith, and also to the framing of a life acceptable to

God; and in this respect *it is expressly commanded by God
that nothing be either added to or taken from the same*
(emphasis mine).[10]

HERE WE STAND

The church has a place of security in which to stand in
this very difficult time: on biblical authority. It is the same
place Luther stood: *Sola scriptura*.[11] This was the standard when the writers of the great confessions were seeking to arrive at clarity and truth. It was doubly true when
Luther spoke out and when the Barmen Declaration was
written against Hitlerism. It is also true today when moral
confusion and chaos are rampant. The church in our time
must rethink and clarify its commitment to the authority of
Scripture and how that authority functions in the life of
the church.

It seems incredible to imagine, after reading the above
statements, that a General Assembly of the United Presbyterian Church could receive the following recommendation from a task force that has studied for fifteen months:
"No phrase within the Constitution can be construed
explicitly to prohibit the ordination of self-affirming
(avowed) practicing homosexual Christians."[12]

Should that one sentence ever be adopted, the classical
application of all biblical passages discussing homosexual
acts would be set aside, much basic biblical theology
would be set aside, and the witness of the Fathers of the
church from ancient to modern times—many of whom
gave their lives for the preservation of the faith—would be
declared null and void.

7

Sloppy Agape
or Liberating Love

THE SAME SCRIPTURE that teaches homosexual acts are sinful and contrary to God's will calls all Christians to love the way Jesus loved. We cannot affirm Scripture where we want to without yielding to it where we need to.

CLARIFYING THE DEBATE

The issue is not whether we are to love homosexuals. That is not optional. The debate is not between those for homosexuals and those against homosexuals. The argument within the mainline church is not whether God loves homosexuals, or whether practicing homosexuals are persons of infinite worth for whom Christ died.

There are those who want to make that the issue. And there are those who want to define the problem by saying, "If you don't agree that the homosexual lifestyle is good, then you don't love us."

The reason we cannot accept this definition of the problem is that while we know God is love, He is also *just* and does not accept homosexual practice as good. God Himself, who is love, is the only one who can define the *meaning* of love.

There are those who approach the issue from the opposite point of view. They say, "If you say the homosexual lifestyle is good, then you don't love *us*." Here I am not quoting heterosexuals. I am referring to homosexuals who are being healed. And I want to underscore that there are *many* such persons. There are not nearly as many as there ought to be, but there are many homosexuals who are finding a new life in Christ and are deeply grateful that some Christians loved them enough to call them to repentance and faith.

Again, let me emphasize that the issue in the debates raging within all mainline denominations is not whether God loves sinners, not whether we are called to love homosexual persons, but rather, *what does it mean to love such persons.*

SEXUAL DRIVES AND SEX ACTS

All of us are sexual beings. As such, we are physically attracted to other persons. For the overwhelming majority that attraction is for persons of the opposite sex and has to be dealt with at two levels: that of the mind where the attraction begins, and that of the will where the decision to act is made.

The temptation is not sinful. It is neutral. Lingering on the temptation leads to fantasizing and to the act of lusting and some times to physical sexual activity. Both the act of lusting and the physical expression are sinful (see Matt. 5:27,28).

For the homosexual, the attraction is for persons of the same sex. That attraction or temptation is not in and of itself sinful. The decision to linger longingly or lustfully upon the thought and the decision to yield and act it out are sinful. Such acts are contrary to the divine intention for Man as male and female.

Apart from such sexual acts, the homosexual person is a sinner for the same reasons, not more and not less, than the rest of us. We are all caught up in the same net of rebellion, and we all have chosen our own special reper-

toire out of the seemingly endless variety of ways to avo.
the holy will of God.

THE BIG QUESTION

Now let us ask the question: Is there "no room" for the
homosexual in the kingdom of God, and therefore, no
room in the church? Scripture says both no and yes. All
sinners are welcome at the Cross, but only repentant sinners are invited to become members of Christ's church.
Calvin commented, "The wicked do, indeed, inherit the
kingdom of God, but only after they have been turned to
the Lord in true repentance and justified after their conversion and so cease to be wicked."[1] Scripture says no to
the avowed, practicing, and unrepentant homosexual just
as it says no to the practicing, unrepentant adulterer, rob-
ber, or idolator. But the answer is yes to the homosexual
who, by the grace and love of God and the prayers and
support of the Christian community, will repent of his or
her behavior, turn to Christ, and seek God's power for a
new lifestyle of wholeness.

When God says such acts are sinful in His sight and
contrary to His intention, is it loving for us to tell such
persons that their active sexual conduct is not sinful?
Should we tell them that it is really okay, and even good?
In fact, should we tell them that because it is good and can
bless us all, we ought to ordain them?

Is this the loving thing to do? I think not. That is sloppy
agape, not liberating love. That is careless and shallow
love, love without responsibility, love without accountability, love that does not liberate.

The church cannot bend at this point and still retain its
integrity as being Christian. On the one hand, it must
insist that homosexuals make a clean break with such
behavior while accepting them with non-judgmental
love. To some this seems cruel and unfeeling. Why should

73

we deny these people the only kind of sexual love they can experience? Let us correct that erroneous idea. We are not the ones denying them. Their definition of love is not only unbiblical, it's trivial.

C. S. Lewis in *The Problem of Pain* made some appropriate statements. He referred to the scriptural analogy between the love of God for a man and the love of a man for a woman. The truth in this analogy of bridegroom and bride, Lewis said, is "to emphasize . . . that Love, in its own nature, demands the perfecting of the beloved, that mere 'kindness' which tolerates anything except suffering in its object is, in that respect, at the opposite pole from love."

God is committed to nothing less than restoring in us the image broken in the Fall. Because of this, His "love is more sensitive than hatred itself to every blemish in the beloved . . . of all powers he forgives most, but he condones least: he is pleased with little, but demands all."

Lewis concludes, "To ask that God's love should be content with us as we are is to ask that God should cease to be God: because He is what He is, His love must, in the nature of things, be impeded and repelled by certain stains in our present character, and because He already loves us He must labour to make us loveable."[2]

Being a Christian homosexual first of all requires a complete break from homosexual acts. That will undoubtedly bring pain, frustration, and loneliness. We must be aware of that. But just because it hurts does not mean it is unloving. Radical surgery is often painful. But then during the lengthy process of surgery and healing, the church must give considerable emotional and spiritual support to such persons.

Likewise the church cannot and must not ordain homosexuals as pastors and elders unless they have first made this break with their lifestyle and have made significant strides toward the redirection of their orientation. To do less would be to default our responsibility as guardians of the flock. It is not that the homosexual is any more a sinner than the rest of us pastors and elders who struggle with the more "mainline" sins. We also must come to terms with *our* sins in relation to *our* ordination. I cannot stress this too much. We cannot call homosexuals to repentance and victory over their besetting sin without acknowledging before God our own besetting sin and the "log in our own eye."

When God calls specific acts sinful and says persons who do them need to repent, how is it possible for us to say it isn't so? If the church were to change its position about homosexual acts being sinful and about ordination, practicing homosexuals would be the losers. They are the ones who would have lost the most, because they would have lost their one possibility for healing and wholeness. They would be led into a false and shallow sense of security that is no security. Jeremiah spoke against such a backdrop:

> . . . from prophet to priest,
> every one deals falsely.
> They have healed the wound of
> my people lightly,
> saying, "Peace, peace,"
> when there is no peace.
> Were they ashamed when they
> committed abomination?
> No, they were not at all ashamed;
> they did not know how to blush.
> (Jer. 6:13–15)

Paul did not originate the truth that "the unrighteous will not inherit the kingdom of God" (see 1 Cor. 6:9). The Holy Spirit did, and He speaks the same message throughout Scripture. Jesus said it a hundred different ways:

"Don't say to me Lord, Lord, and not do what I say . . .
Depart from me, I never knew you . . . (Matt. 7:21–23,
paraphrased).

"If you do what I say, you will build on a rock.
If you don't do what I say, you will build on the sand . . .
(Matt. 7:24–26, paraphrased).

"If you don't forgive from your heart, neither will your
Father in heaven forgive you . . . (Matt. 6:14, paraphrased).

"Inasmuch as you have done it unto one of the least of these
my brethren you have done it unto me . . . (Matt. 25:40,
paraphrased).

"Go, and sin no more . . . (John 8:11, KJV).

"Do not think that I have come to bring peace on earth; I
have not come to bring peace, but a sword" (Matt. 10:34; see
also Matt. 10:15ff).

Can our love do any less? The issue before us is not
what do a few texts of Scripture say, but what does God's
total revelation say? The message is clear.*

---

*An excellent book for further study on God's grace as costly and
powerful grace is Richard F. Lovelace, *The Church and
Homosexuality*. (To be published by Fleming H. Revell, summer 1978.)

8

Clinics and Clerics

MEDICAL AND PSYCHOLOGICAL RESEARCH

IN DEALING WITH the gay crisis in our society, it is vitally important for us to be aware of what is being said in the research lab—and why. To better understand what the medical and psychological experts are saying about homosexuality, the approach of this chapter will be
  (1) to look at some of the different approaches to studying human behavior,
  (2) to consider different conclusions these researchers reach because of their philosophic presuppositions,
  (3) to look at the implications of this data for a biblical Christian approach to homosexual morality,
  (4) to answer some of the questions most asked by the gay establishment who regard homosexuality as a "gift of God," and
  (5) to suggest a model for diagnosing the cause(s) of homosexual behavior with implications for "healings" or "treatment."
One of the most important and frequent questions asked of social scientists is, "Is homosexual behavior caused by heredity or environment, or is it a free choice?" The school of thought in which the scientist was trained will certainly influence his answer. Therefore, let us consider

the most prominent schools of thought and how they explain homosexual behavior.

GENETIC PREDISPOSITION

Karl Ulrichs hypothesized "a female soul in a male body,"[1] and Dr. Richard Von Krafft-Ebing, a pre-Freudian sexologist, postulated in 1887 that homosexuality was genetically caused. It is interesting to note that Dr. Krafft-Ebing's patients corroborated his theories, and he concluded that homosexuals possessed the "soul" or "brain center" of the opposite sex.[2]

After these popular conclusions of ninety years ago had laid a specific foundation to explain homosexual behavior, many studies were done in an attempt to correlate heredity and homosexuality.* From the data thus gathered, one would conclude that a person may, at birth, have "some hidden predisposition ... that makes him or her *more vulnerable* [emphasis mine] to differentiate a psychosexual identity as a homosexual—not in any preordained, automatic, or mechanistic sense, but only if the social environment happens to provide the right confluence of circumstances."[3]

Those who would place homosexual behavior solely in the genetic code as a predetermined behavior pattern seem to have little data to support them. However, one continues to hear about "constitutional homosexuality" as a school of thought. Such a model is supported by many homosexuals, including Troy Perry who charges that a former homosexual now in a heterosexual marriage is living in sin. Reverend Perry's rationale is that according to Romans 1:26, the former homosexual had changed his

---

*For the reader interested in a more in-depth treatment on the question of innate homosexuality, it is suggested you read Dr. William White's paper listed in the bibliography, as well as other bibliographic sources.

natural (inborn, genetic, constitutional) sex preference (i.e., homosexual) for one that is now unnatural (i.e., heterosexual).[4] Thus, genetic predisposition to *either* homosexuality or heterosexuality is a touchstone of some gay theology and gay psychology, even though it is not supported by research data.*

ENVIRONMENT DETERMINES BEHAVIOR

A second school of thought that looks at all behavior from a deterministic basis is Freudianism or classic psychoanalysis. Although Freudian analysis is deterministic, it supports *environmental* determinism rather than *biological* or chemical determinism. Freud believed that if the normal psychosexual development of children was hindered at a certain stage, the result would be a homosexual preference. This hindrance was called a "perversion," and, since all persons have heterosexual, homosexual, and bisexual tendencies, Freud stated that one should not be shocked if such a thing were to occur. If a change were desired, long psychoanalysis would be required to unblock the neurotic fixation. Above all, Freud taught that such sexual perversion should not be considered a crime or a sin but simply the result of developmental difficulties.

An important neo-Freudian theorist who has written extensively on this matter is Irving Bieber. Bieber contends that early childhood experiences, not genetic predetermination, are keys to understanding homosexuality. It is from Bieber and others that the *family model* of the homosexual emerges, showing a distant, hostile, and cold

---

*In an address on February 13, 1978, in Chicago, Dr. Aahmes Overton reported that Dr. William Masters told the Presbyterian Task Force that some physiological and chemical changes in a person may result from homosexual behavior rather than cause it.

father and a smothering mother. He concludes that homosexuality is a "pathologic bisocial, psychosexual adaption consequent to pervasive fears surrounding the expression of heterosexual impulses." In his view "every homosexual is in reality a latent heterosexual."[5]

Who would challenge the importance of early childhood relationships, especially those of the nuclear family? I find my own experiences agreeing in great part with Beiber's conclusions. An acquaintance named Sara exemplifies it well.

Sara's family life fit well into the model of a distant father and a mother who "wore the pants in the family." Father was often gone, and Sara saw him only on rare and somewhat terrifying occasions. Mother protected Sara from her father and to this day she has difficulty talking with him. In addition, her father has an authoritarian personality, which adds to the rejection syndrome. These early experiences caused Sara to react with fear toward male relationships, and she had an early desire for intimacy with members of the same sex. These began in grade school and continued until her conversion to Jesus Christ at the age of twenty-seven.

Of course Freudian and neo-Freudian theories have dominated Western thought regarding behavior for several decades. As a result, much behavior formerly considered sinful and/or criminal has been reclassified as either sick or morally neutral. But in any case, the home environment rather than the individual himself is considered responsible for resultant behavior. Since such people are innocent of responsibility, they must be "cured" rather than punished.

CHILDHOOD CONDITIONING

Possibly the most important psychological theorist of the past two decades is B. F. Skinner. A direct philosophical descendant of Pavlov and Watson, Skinner categorically asserts that all present behavior is a result of complex patterns of conditioning received in childhood. Thus Skinner is, like Freud, a behavioral determinist, but one who would see the possibility of "reconditioning" persons through a series of rewards and punishments and thereby causing the person to desire a different behavior pattern.

My experience with a girl I'll call Sally, as well as with others, confirms the behavioral hypothesis that rewarded behavior will continue and grow stronger, and punished behavior will tend to become extinct. Sally worked professionally in a large midwestern city for several years following college graduation. Her social life was somewhat restricted, for she felt uncomfortable around men.

Then she met Rebecca, a lesbian of several years, and became involved as a friend, then as a companion—and finally she became Rebecca's partner sexually, financially, and emotionally. They lived together for over seven years, after which time they both came to know and love Jesus Christ as their Savior.

The transition was difficult for both of them. But Sally's behavior was more easily changed as it was more profoundly the result of conditioning than was Rebecca's. As we sought to reinforce a normal heterosexual viewpoint and deal with her fear of men, Sally's disentanglement was completed.

Since Skinner and his followers assume that *all* present behavior is the result of past conditioning, therapeutic approaches focus almost exclusively on behavioral modification.

Several reports indicate that behavioral modification techniques are quite successful in changing homosexual preferences to heterosexual preferences. This implies, at least, that the behavior is strongly influenced by conditioning.[6]

HUMANISM

No report on homosexual research would be complete without a brief look at the "third force" in psychology after Freud and Skinner. This third force is called by many names but will be referred to here as "humanistic psychology." Carl Rogers epitomizes the nondirective branch of this movement, which assumes that man is basically good and simply needs to find for himself the proper way to live. Rogerian counseling sees homosexuality as a personal choice with neither moral content nor predeterministic tendencies.

A more directive form of humanistic psychology is followed by Dr. William Glasser of Reality Therapy fame. Dr. Glasser stresses responsibility for one's behavior without regard for the past experiences of childhood or parenting. One simply decides what he wants to do and does it. (Glasser probably would not see homosexuality as a sin or a sickness, but as a preferred lifestyle—as would Rogers.)

The life and writings of Albert Ellis are well known. Ellis enjoys helping people break out of the moral myths about sex (and other issues) that cause them anguish, and to make attitudes toward sex "rational." Hence, he is the creator of Rational Emotive Therapy (RET). Ellis proposes that people have emotional difficulties not because of their genes or their parents, but because of their irrational ideas of what is moral and acceptable. That which the Scripture calls sexually immoral and sinful, Ellis calls good and acceptable. Any notions of adultery or homosexuality being sinful are irrational according to him. Thus, dispose of your stupid, self-defeating, irrational ideas about sexual behavior, and you will be all right.

I am reminded of a person who went to see a psychologist because he was agonizing over his homosexual tendencies and the resultant guilt and shame. George had led

Christian groups at many campuses and churches. A fine musician, he was in demand for concerts in churches and youth groups.

The counselor practiced RET and told George that his notions of morality were irrational, that his parents were old-fashioned Victorian prudes, and that he would never be happy until he expressed himself in a gay lifestyle.

The lifestyle change was immediate and apparent. The hostility toward his parents that had until then been repressed was thrust to the surface and George made every effort to punish them for their "irrational" behavior. His already great tendency toward self-centeredness became overwhelming and he "rationally" did his own thing with little regard for others. What a tragic result.

THE MORAL / SPIRITUAL MODEL

Another approach to the causality of homosexuality is the moral/spiritual model. Traditionally, some persons have taken Romans 1:28–32 to indicate that the root cause of homosexuality is "alienation from God through idolatry" and will disappear upon conversion and repentance. Two present-day Christian leaders recently stated that anyone continuing to struggle with homosexual sins is more than likely not a Christian. This, it seems to me, essentially reduces homosexual behavior to a single factor—spiritual condition—and when that is changed, so proponents of this view contend, so will the behavior. I believe this is an oversimplification of cause and solution.

There are other Christian groups who take a similar philosophic stance but come out at a different place. These people see a demonic cause in addition to the moral/spiritual condition. Thus, not only conversion and repentance are needed, but one must also be delivered or exorcised. These approaches to homosexuality are not related to psychological data but are important in filling

83

out the range of philosophic systems for approaching this issue.

What are the implications of the above studies and the resultant approaches to homosexual behavior? Hardly anyone seems to agree with the strictly Freudian position any more (see Tripp,[7] Beiber,[8] McNeill,[9] and Bergler[10]), and several writers suggest a multi-modality approach to both cause and treatment.

For example, Dr. David Lester states that there are

> a wide range of possible etiological factors [causes] deter-mining sexual choice. There is some evidence from twin studies for a genetic component, although the data have not reached the level of complexity required before confidence can be placed in the results. There is some evidence of physiological, and in particular endocrinological, factors. Here the current research is contradictory. . . .
>
> Evidence on central nervous system involvement is quite poor. Evidence for the influence of the parents is good, should the results be found to be reliable, even when differences in psychopathology of the different groups being held are held constant.[11]

It is key to remember that because of differences among various schools of thought, conclusions by respective proponents based on a single study could vary greatly. As Lester states, "It is important to be aware of the degree of bias that is present in research and theorizing about sexual deviations."[12]

In this context, I am reminded of a man in his forties who was married and had carefully hidden his gay life-style from his family, friends, and professional colleagues. He had great fears of relating to women sexually. He suffered from performance anxiety and often was unable to hold an erection until ejaculation. This failure caused increased anxiety and stress which led him back into the gay lifestyle he had practiced as a youth.

Upon receiving Christ as Savior, this man shared his dilemma with me. An analysis of his past revealed a family pattern that conformed to the strong mother/weak father hypothesis. In addition, when he was six years old, he was caught and shamed greatly, as well as beaten, for fondling a female playmate. Other factors included his mother's bathing him in a way that aroused his normal sexual urges and the resultant shame, and an older uncle who regularly caressed and fondled him from age four to age thirteen.

Despite all these factors, and a very active homosexual lifestyle in college and after, this man sought and maintained a very happy heterosexual relationship with his first wife. During that marriage he had no homosexual relationships or fantasy life. However, this marriage had taken place while he was overseas in the military, and upon his return home the relationship was severed.

His subsequent marriage to a sexually inhibited woman brought back many of the old fears of failure and of hurting a woman he greatly loved. One gay encounter led to another and before long he was finding it easier and easier to have his sexual needs met by men, rather than by his wife.

In this case, as in many others I have known, we see multiple causes for homosexual behavior in its genesis and reinforcement: (1) the classical parental relationships of a weak father and a smothering mother; (2) insensitive parents who shamed and punished him for heterosexual testing (this fits both the psychoanalytic model and the Skinner model); (3) an insensitive mother who aroused her son to erections and sexual fantasy (a Freudian field day here); (4) an uncle whom the man loved engaged him in pleasurable homosexual behavior (a tremendously powerful reinforcer of that behavior both physically and emotionally); (5) a frigid, unresponsive wife who aroused all of his old fears and anxieties. And there is nothing to say that this man might not have a genetic tendency toward homosexuality. Thus, studied opinions on him could vary greatly. And the above story and analysis reveals my own bias: Homosexual behavior is, like *all* abiding and habitual behavior, the result of many factors and causes.

THE GAY REACTION

Some specific questions related to this research naturally follow. For example, some members of the gay establishment contend, as noted earlier, that homosexuals are created that way by God (i.e., genetically). Thus, they say, constitutional homosexuality is the "natural" sexual preference for those persons. To change them, they say, would be a violation of Scripture (see Rom. 1:26,27) and would be thereby sinful. Others point out that God created homosexuals with this orientation, they cannot change, and thus God would be unjust in holding them to be sinful.

Genetic and endocrinal research is very inconclusive now. But *what if* the time comes when studies are conclusive in showing causality? If that happens, the charge that some homosexuals were created that way would be substantiated scientifically.

A CHRISTIAN RESPONSE

The Christian must give thoughtful answers to these questions. In the first instance, it should be noted that the Romans passage does *not* state that "The women had changed *their* natural" sexual functioning for an unnatural, as some gay spokespersons assert. Instead, the passage reads, "changed *the* natural" with a definite emphasis upon the fact that there is *a* natural way and there is an unnatural way to have sexual relationships.

Also, this reference to "natural" uses not the *individuals* involved as its standard for comparison but the *created order* as God intended it to be. (As Helmut Thielicke states, "The homosexual must always understand himself in terms of his disparity with the 'normal' polarity of the sexes and to this extent also remains bound to it.")[13]

The second issue concerns how the church could hold a "constitutional" or congenital homosexual responsible for committing sin. Although I believe this situation to be a rare occurrence, if it occurs only once we must reply. It is not difficult to imagine a genetic or chromosomal defect in this area any more than in a number of other areas. A large percentage of our population suffer from birth defects of one kind or another. All such defects are the result of a sinful, fallen universe and are not the "normal" condition.

The question follows, then, should we hold such a person responsible for his behavior? Think for a moment— can a person with congenital blindness ever be charged with a related sin?

Our answer is yes and no. A blind person is not and should not be considered a sinner for his constitutional blindness. On the other hand, were he to drive a car I would insist that he be adjudged guilty of wrong.

Similarly, if my wife were to fall into a deep coma today, and we were unable to continue our active heterosexual relationship, I could call upon the community to excuse my having sex with other women on the basis of my "constitutional heterosexuality." I could claim that God had created me this way and that it is grossly unfair for me to be judged guilty for simply doing that which comes naturally. But Scripture doesn't allow that option.

In my acquaintance are numerous single men and women. Some are divorced, others have lost their mates through death, and some have never married. Each has a normal sexual nature. Yet, I could not, as a loving pastor, affirm their out-of-wedlock sexual encounters.

It is crucial to differentiate between *condition* and *behavior*. The Scripture says that we are all children of wrath, and it is my experience that some of us come from the womb angry, rebellious, and hostile. Those persons might properly be called "constitutionally hostile." However, were they to ignore the moral restraints of that condition and fantasize murderous thoughts or attack another person in word or deed, I would hold them accountable for sinful behavior. Jesus made it clear that our behavior in thought and in deed has a moral content, even if that behavior came from "our father the Devil," as He accused the Pharisees.

It is my conviction that the homosexual constitution is indeed rare, and even if it does exist, we ought to do all we can to change that condition, just as we would do all we could to bring wholeness to the genetically lame, blind, or deaf. I assert that if and when constitutional homosexuality is discovered, I would do all that I could do, with God's help, to remedy this result of the fallen condition.

THE GENETIC QUESTION—A RATIONALIZATION?

Another aspect of this matter that must be faced by us and by the gay establishment is the fact that "homosexuality as a genetic condition" is often used as a rationalization to allow one to justify his behavior. In my view, that is an understandable, even reasonable position to take. Neither the church nor the psychotherapeutic establishment has offered much hope for anything but rejection, shame, and pain. Given these circumstances, any reasonable person would search for a rationale to explain his dilemma and to reduce the awful load of guilt, shame, and self-hate.

It is also common knowledge among members of the helping professions that defense mechanisms serve quite a useful purpose of protecting the ego of a person from being completely overwhelmed. Another "truism" is that very often persons in emotional and spiritual agony fight hard to hold on to their problem, whether it is depression, anxiety, or sexual deviance. Thus, gays and others may cry out for help but in reality fight all attempts to help them change.

Aware of these issues, I call on members of the Christian community to recognize the importance of defense mechanisms such as denial and rationalization which make the genetic condition argument very attractive. When one sees the deviousness of his own defense mechanisms, there is much more likelihood of positive change.

This was true of Bart, who came to see me after committing his life to Christ. Bart felt sure that he was a constitutional homosexual whom God would not hold accountable since "in His providence He created me this way." After many long hours of talking, praying, and agonizing over this matter (he was one of the first alleged constitutional homosexuals I knew), I challenged his rationalizing and manipulative attempts to get me to agree with his self-delusional system. Although many other problems existed, that confrontation freed Bart to see himself more honestly and to relate to God more openly.

TREATMENT

Although reports vary considerably, one usually hears that few, if any, true homosexuals really change through psychotherapy. This difficulty in achieving permanent change is one of the arguments often advanced by gays as a defense of their lifestyle. Although I think that the success rate is often greater than gays admit, here are several reasons why I believe that success in the past has been as limited as it has been:

1. Research is usually done on persons who are not Christians and thus do not have the motivating, empowering, sanctifying life of the Holy Spirit to assist their growth.
2. Non-Christians (and Christians) have rarely had a reconciling, loving community to support their growth and change. Deep, caring, loving responsible fellowship in the Holy Spirit is life-changing.
3. Little research and discussion on the multiple treatments necessary for achieving change has been done in the area of sexual deviance; however much is being learned in recent years about treatment of the whole person.
4. Frankly, success in treating homosexuals is as good as or better than the success rate for other behavioral difficulties.[14] Alcoholism, depression, schizophrenia, and anxiety—all have had a stubborn resistance to traditional Freudian psychoanalysis which requires several hundred fifty-dollar sessions to get at the root of most problems.

   It is my conviction that the success rate for treatment of homosexuals will increase dramatically in the next few years as a result of (a) better treatment interventions by therapists in general as a result of better research, more wholistic approaches to the problem, and greater skills in providing therapy, and (b) the increased concern, knowledge, and skill of Christians.

   Several therapists report a very high success rate with homosexuals now if their motivation for change is great.[15] And many Christian ministries report good success with gays who want to be straight.

5. I suspect that the awful shame surrounding homosexuality has kept many persons "in the closet" and away from seeking help. Now that things are more in the open, hopefully people will seek assistance earlier, and we will be able to respond accordingly.

6. The cost of change has been prohibitive in the past. Few could afford the enormous cost of seeing a psychoanalyst. Now that the church is responding, perhaps that will be overcome.

The majority report of the Presbyterian Task Force makes two statements that are not supported by the facts. First, they state that "Homosexuality . . . is a strong, enduring, not consciously chosen and usually irreversible affectional attraction to and preference for persons of the same sex."

Although a homosexual lifestyle is strong and enduring, it is certainly chosen. Anyone familiar with the research data on this matter knows that, although unconscious drives are powerful, one has a conscious choice to make in whether that drive is acted out or not.

In addition, the statement that it is "usually irreversible" is simply contrary to the data and experience of Christians who take their call to ministry seriously. It is interesting that even the majority report uses the term "irreversible," which explicitly means that a behavior is either forward or backward. Thus, they are admitting that movement toward a homosexual lifestyle and the resultant behavior is hard to reverse.

The second statement notes that the biblical "passages must be placed within . . . the context of expanding empirical knowledge. . . ." My first reaction is, what *new* empirical knowledge? The new empirical data seem to suggest conclusions *contrary* to the majority report and consistent with the biblical view. I strongly object to the use of the myth of scientific objectivity as a support of gay rights. Science is *not* objective in the first place, and second, there is no new data to indicate genetic homosexuality. To the contrary, as data emerge they show additional reasons why evangelical Christians should rejoice in the hope of additional means to bring wholeness to broken people.

THE CHRISTIAN MODEL

The model for a Christian perspective in ministry to the homosexual must treat the *whole* person and not simply one or a few of the parts. The model must seriously accept the biblical emphasis on moral responsibility in thought and deed as well as its emphasis on spiritual realities. It must be applicable by the church and be proven in its practical application.

In the final analysis, when the Christian faces the *contradictory* claims and conclusions of the scientists and researchers, he must always return to his bedrock task and remember that believers are not called primarily to the "adjusted" or "socially acceptable." In fact, that which is called adjusted or socially acceptable by definition of a culture (and even its learned societies such as the American Bar Association and the American Psychiatric Association) is often at great variance with the standard of Christ. We are called rather to "not be conformed to [the *Weltanschauung* of] this present world but to be transformed by the renewing of our minds."

In that regard, let Christians on all sides of this issue remember that we are to choose righteousness, not necessarily respectability. As a pastor I must call for righteousness and justice, regardless of ease or personal compassion. The gospel must comfort the afflicted but afflict the comfortable. Righteousness, not research, will decide where the church must stand.

9

Gay Agony:
The Real Paradox

PSYCHIC PAIN is as real as physical pain and perhaps more debilitating. Some of the studies in psychosomatic medicine point out the very high rate of real physical illness resulting from emotional and spiritual pain.[1] As Christians we have no problem in recognizing this as clear biblical teaching. Persons are whole—not parts—and when one aspect is affected, so are all the others.

AGONY FOR ALL

This is especially true for the deepest aspect—the heart or spirit. "A man's spirit will endure sickness; but a broken spirit who can bear?" (Prov. 18:14).

It is precisely to these persons, the broken hearted and those bruised in spirit, that we Christians have been called to minister. Our Messiah said that He was anointed " '... to preach good news to the poor .... proclaim release to the captives and recovering of sight to the blind, to set at liberty those who are oppressed, to proclaim the acceptable year of the Lord' " (Luke 4:18,19).

As a pastor I have listened to literally hundreds of hurting, despondent, shame-ridden, and fearful people whose problems included frigidity, grief over the loss of a family member, alienated families, alcoholism, adultery, chronic depression, and more. I testify that their pain is real and that the church of Jesus Christ is called to administer the healing balm of Gilead.

We have fancy theological, sociological, and psychological terminology. But whatever it is that we do to attempt to hide ourselves from God, from others, and even from ourselves, the result for us is separation, anxiety, enmity, strife—in a word, *agony*. Feel the agony in this incredible confession:

PLEASE HEAR WHAT I'M SAYING

Don't be fooled by me.
Don't be fooled by the face I wear.
For I wear a mask, a thousand masks,
   masks that I'm afraid to take off,
   and none of them are me.
Pretending is an art that's second nature with me,
   but don't be fooled, for God's sake,
   don't be fooled.
I give you the impression that I'm secure,
   that all is sunny and unruffled with me,
   within as well as without,
   that confidence is my name
   and coolness is my game,
   that the water's calm, and I'm in command,
   and that I need no one.
But don't believe me.
   Please.

My surface may seem smooth, but my surface is my mask,
   my ever-varying and ever-concealing mask.
Beneath lies no smugness, no complacence.
Beneath dwells the real me in confusion, in fear, in aloneness.
That's why I frantically create a mask to hide behind,
   a nonchalant, sophisticated facade,
   to help me pretend,
   to shield me from the glance that knows.

But such a glance is precisely my salvation.
And I know it.
That is if it's followed by acceptance, if it's followed by love.
It's the only thing that can liberate me, from myself,
    from my own self-built prison walls,
    from the barriers that I so painstakingly erect.
It's the only thing that will assure me of what I can't assure
    myself,
    that I'm really worth something.
But I don't tell you this. I don't care. I'm afraid to.
I'm afraid your glance won't be followed by acceptance and
    love.
I'm afraid that deep down I'm nothing,
    that I'm just no good,
    and that you will see this and reject me.

But you've got to help me.
You've got to hold out your hand
    even when that's the last thing I seem to want, or need.
Only you can call me to aliveness.
Only you can wipe away from my eyes the blank stare of the
    breathing dead.
Each time you're kind, and gentle, and encouraging,
    each time you try to understand because you really care,
    my heart begins to grow wings, very small wings,
    very feeble wings, but wings.
I want you to know how important you are to me,
    how you can be a creator of the person that is me if you
    choose to.
Please choose to.

It will not be easy for you.
A long conviction of worthlessness builds strong walls,
The nearer you approach me, the blinder I may strike back.
It's irrational, but despite what the books may say about
    man, I am irrational.
I fight against the very thing that I cry out for.
    But I am told that love is stronger than strong walls,
    and in this lies my hope.
    My only hope.

Who am I, you may wonder? I am someone you know very
well.

For I am every man you meet and I am every woman you
meet.

—Anonymous[2]

HOW DO WE HEAR?

It is obvious that I am setting the stage for better comprehension of the agony of homosexuals—practicing or
closeted. The barriers to our hearing are great. It will take
hard work for the typical Christian community to *hear*,
and to really *feel* the deep psychic pain of a group of
people whose moral and theological stances are so at
variance with our own.

What is causing us to resist hearing? Are we threatened
or angry about the possibility that we might be called to
show compassion for people we find ugly, sinful, and
repulsive? Yes! However, God calls you and me to show
compassion and redeeming love toward homosexual men
and women.

Take a closer look at your barriers to hearing. Is it
stereotypic thinking or the notion that you have nothing
to learn from such a group of people? Is it fear that they
may be more right than you believed and that hearing
would force you to look more closely at your position?

Perhaps it is a defensive move to cover up some personal besetting sin that you are struggling with. Or even
more frightening, maybe you are not as sure as you would
like to be of your own femininity or masculinity. Whatever
the barriers, I ask you in the name of our Lord to open your
pains, and sins, and fears to Him and to others. Can you
join me in this prayer?

Lord, I want to stop and look. Make me honest. Help me
take off my mask. God, you know how often I've wanted to

knock those walls down. I've hoped someone would notice and gently help me remove them. Why did I say those words? Why did he say those words? They hurt us both so much. Please forgive and reconcile us.

You know that inside I feel like a little boy dealing with a subject beyond my capacity. You know that my feelings of inadequacy are real. You also know that my inadequacy is real. Don't let me appear more knowledgeable than I really am. Don't let me think more highly of myself than I ought. Don't let me fear saying what needs to be said.

Help me to face my own sin honestly. Help them too, Lord. But then move us all beyond our sin to your Cross, to your forgiveness.

Lord, I want to love the people you love and to love them your way.

GAY AGONY IS FOR REAL

This is the real paradox: To be "gay" is seldom to be gay. It's like smoking more, but enjoying it less. It's like saying "gay is beautiful" enough times and loud enough and enthusiastically enough to try to make yourself—and others—believe it. And yet for many, if not most, to be gay is to know almost constant pain and fear and frustration and self-hate. Let me discuss a few of the characteristics of this agony in some detail.

FEAR OF DETECTION

The term for a covert homosexual is a "closeted homosexual." When gays decide to be open and overt in their lifestyle, they are said to "come out of the closet."

What does it mean to hide in the closet: Think with me, what does it do to *us* to live a double life? Like the person in the poem *Please Hear What I'm Saying*, the vast majority of us experience a great gulf between what we reveal on the outside, and what we are really like on the

97

inside—even if our besetting sin is "not all that bad." We fear being known; thus, we play the game of revealing only what we want others to see. We learn quickly how to say and do the right thing.

It is a common, almost universal condition for all of us to have some closets we don't want others to open. But this is the *total* life of most practicing homosexuals. They are living a double life virtually day and night. The fear of detection is the constant fear of most closeted gays. If it were not for that fear, they would have come out long ago. This is one of the cries I heard:

> For thirty years I've guarded my steps. I've never let any heterosexual know me as I really am. I've never shared my problem before. My whole life has been filled with deception. I can't stand the thought of what it would do to my family or my job or my friendships.

Have you ever seen the pain and the release when such a person has come out of the closet and made himself known? Have you ever worked with someone who is still in the closet and fearful to come out? When we see the depth of his struggle, fear, and anguish, we want to guard his secret with total loyalty. And we can better understand the relief he feels when he makes himself known.

Malcolm Boyd, the Episcopal priest, came out of the closet publicly in 1976 at the second annual convention of Integrity, Incorporated (the Episcopal gay caucus) held at Trinity Episcopal Church in San Francisco.

> Racked with emotional reminiscence and remorse, Boyd read to the convention a poignant letter from a gay priest to a gay monk (an excerpt from Boyd's *Book of Days*). They were deeply in love and separated. Because of vocation, there was no chance of fellowship. The letter, written several years after the separation, read—

"We have lived, holding one another in a rested state of being. I could only assume the crises and decisions, the sadnesses and fulfillments, within your life and never know them.

"But I wanted to know them.

"It was the desire for this knowing which I had to relinquish. I finally did."

"The priest," Boyd confessed, "was me. After such an experience of loss, utter loneliness and the abyss, what can one do?" he asked. . . .

As he approached the end of his address, reciting prayers newly composed, experiencing this new covenant within Integrity (fellow gays and gay sympathizers), Boyd's voice broke, his body shook with the overpowering release of his long imprisoned self. His eyes welled with tears and overflowed. The listeners rose to their feet with emotion-packed, identity-filled applause. Then the hugging and more and more applause.[3]

This reveals the release within Malcolm Boyd in finally coming out of the closet. The response of that gathering also reveals they knew what he was going through and experienced it with him. They understood the agony. Many of them had been there or were still there.

An older pastor, a closeted homosexual, was nearing retirement after many years of service. One Sunday he poignantly ended his sermon with a quote from Thornton Wilder, "In love's service, only the wounded can serve." A homosexual who knew of the pastor's problem wrote, "How true it was for him . . . who had suffered in a suffocating closet all his life at the hands of a misunderstanding, insensitive, and often oppressive church and society."

Please do not be defensive about his accusation of the "often oppressive church and society." We have offered condemnation instead of cleansing to persons with all kinds of problems. The church and society are also made up of sinners like us. We are often unloving sinners who add tremendously to the burdens of one another, rather than setting one another free in the grace of Christ.

DETECTION, THEN REJECTION

The fear of rejection for the homosexual is usually so great that telling the family is almost impossible. "If I tell my parents, will they reject me? Will they disown me or fear me or hate me? Will they be harsh or silent? Will they be angry or crushed? Will they blame one another? Can they live with it or will it be destructive to their own relationship?"

For the married gay, the risks are even greater. Should the spouse be told? "What would it do to her?" he asks. "Our relationship has not been all that good. She's already wondered why and felt inadequate. But this could be the final straw. It would crush her. It would break her heart. She would realize that she really never knew me."

And how does the pastor counsel a new Christian who is a homosexual with a spouse of many years? Should he have the person "tell all" or be discrete? Does he advise, "Those old sins are behind the Cross—start anew"? Is gay sex adultery?

These and other equally difficult questions face the serious pastor. I face the tempter who lies to me and says, "Let the gays find sexual fulfillment wherever they can, but don't bother with them—you've got a whole church to lead."

But the love of Christ constrains me to show God's *liberating love* to gay Christians whose painful dilemma is all too apparent to even me.

ALIENATION FROM THE CHURCH

A young gay Presbyterian who seeks ordination has said, "The gay person cannot celebrate her or his feelings in most Christian communities. Usually, for most gay women and men, coming out *in* the church has meant coming out *of* the church. Gay persons are rejected from the church unconsciously and consciously, hatefully and 'lovingly,' blatantly, and latently." [4]

He went on to say, "Gay persons are pushed away from the Lord's table and allowed only the streets, the tea rooms, the bars, the baths, and the gay ghettos. Coming out of the closet, a process the church should be enabling and ennobling, is a process which must be experienced more often in the secular world than in the Christian community." [5]

His analysis agrees with my own. I see far too much of a cultural response toward needy people and far too little tough and sacrificial love that cares enough to talk (and live) repentance and forgiveness in Christ.

Although I agree with this young man's analysis of the experience of gays in the church, I must forcefully disagree with the statement that coming out ought to be "enabling and ennobling" to the gay. Although no orthodox Christian church could support the ethics of a homosexual lifestyle, we *must* respond to gays in a caring and helpful way—showing concern, compassion, and hope for change.

FEAR OF FAILURE

The practicing homosexual usually has heard that homosexual acts are wrong, and has felt within himself that they are wrong. Any overt or covert disobedience of the moral law brings about guilt. Continuing to sin, to transgress the law, brings about an awesome sense of shame and a fear of failure.

One person has described the struggle this way:

> I learned from society, then from the Bible, that homosexuality was a sin. I hoped as a child that it was just a phase through which I was passing. I firmly believed that God could change me, so I fervently prayed for such a change.
>
> I felt guilty every time I fantasized about another boy. Because I believed that one couldn't be both homosexual and Christian, I began to doubt the efficacy of my earlier confession and baptism. So I began repenting and confessing and accepting Jesus all over again. I was converted as often as several times a day. But I was still homosexual. And I still loved God. Despite what society and the church told me, I still experienced God's love for me.
>
> I grew to believe that if God wanted me to be different, God would have made me different in the first place, or changed me in the second place. There were more important things for me to be concerned about in the world than my homosexuality.
>
> So I accepted my homosexuality as "my cross to bear," "a thorn in my flesh" which I could never share with anybody, with which I would have to silently suffer, until the day I died and received my reward in heaven.

I know that this young man is sincere. While I do believe that he can in fact be healed, I also sense that *he* no longer believes that he can. He has sought to know that healing again, and again, and again. For him, it "didn't work." The possiblity of another failure and fear of total disillusionment has led him and many others like him to "forget it."

SELF-ACCEPTANCE

Most of us struggle with self-love, but the gay struggle is of a greater intensity. In much of the literature that has been written, gays seem to put the blame for their lack of self-acceptance on the attitudes of the church and the society. This is undoubtedly *partially* true of the many people who loathe and reject homosexuality and all that surrounds it. Some are in the church and some are in the society. They have been influenced by *both* the church and the society. In addition, the *Bible* has had a profound influence upon the moral values esteemed by people.

However, I also want to make a plea for gays to look more honestly at themselves and more responsibly to the Scriptures. Because the underlying reason for their lack of self-acceptance is sin, and the true moral guilt that comes with it, gays need to know that all of us find it difficult to accept ourselves and love ourselves. We find it most difficult when we are rebelling against God and living in sin.

Gays accuse us of focusing upon their sin and not facing our own. They say, "why don't you face your sins of fornication and adultery as seriously as you want us to face our homosexuality? Why aren't you concerned about your inability to love us the way Jesus calls you to love us? Is that not as serious as our sin?" Yes, it is.

Sin does reach the church. However, when we face our own sins squarely and gratefully accept God's grace, then we are set free to love fellow sinners. So I must say to the homosexual, if you are *truly* concerned over straight people's sins, turn your own sin over to Jesus Christ and then, please come help us! Should I not say the same thing to the rest of us? If we are truly concerned over homosexual sins, let us turn our sin over to Jesus Christ, and then, please come help them!

STRUGGLE FOR LASTING RELATIONSHIPS

Think with me for a moment. What do the deep, lasting relationships in your life mean to you? If you are happily married, how much does the love of your spouse mean to you? If you have children, and if you are in a wholesome relationship with your children, how much do they mean to you? If you are single and have had close friends through the years, friends you count on, how much do they mean to you?

Now, as difficult as this will be, please seek through your imagination to remove every one of those deep, lasting relationships. I would suggest that you remove them one by one and feel the pain that you would know if they died, if they were gone forever.

Many practicing homosexuals are void of these kinds of lasting relationships. They do have other kinds of friendships because of their common life and the pain they share (often secretly), but even those are often difficult. This is by choice, you say. Probably so, but the pain and loneliness are still real.

Norman Pittenger, the Episcopal theologian who recently came out of the closet, wrote an article "The Homosexual Expression of Love." In it, he said,

> Without concerning ourselves with the heterosexual, we can say that homosexuals are driven by their sexual desires (good in themselves) by their desperate loneliness (a terrible reality for many homosexuals), and by social rejection (felt deeply in the homosexual world), to secure *any* opportunity to find sexual release, some kind of companionship, if only for a few minutes or hours, and acceptance of other human beings . . .
>
> For what the homosexual longs for, with a profound and almost frightening intensity, is a relationship with another person which will have about it the quality of some permanence and thus enable him to know the faithfulness and commitment, tenderness, respect for self and others, hopeful expectation, and mutuality in giving-and-receiving . . .
> Anyone who says that homosexuals do *not* yearn for this

only demonstrates that he has never known any homosexuals who have opened up to him their deepest self.[6]

This powerful and revealing personal statement from a gay writer must move us to tears for the man and woman locked in their lonely lives of desperation. The gay can never know that physical, mental, and spiritual unity of "becoming one flesh," for even when heterosexual intercourse is experienced, they are, in reality, somewhere else in mind and emotion. It is only by sheer will power that most gays have heterosex.

Pittenger's statement must come close to describing in contemporary terminology something of what God meant when He said that the penalty for sin was death. As companions in the common human condition of sin, we have some "fellow feelings" with the agony another man feels in the midst of his dilemma. However, the stark loneliness and hopelessness of the gay is somehow beyond our comprehension.

Why then am I sharing this? Because there's a great danger that we will feel a need to refute their testimony up front, rather than to really hear them. I found that need in myself when Pittenger said, "homosexuals are driven by their sexual desires (good in themselves)." I wanted to interrupt immediately and say, "No! They are not good in themselves. You want to say that they are good in themselves because then you feel justified. You want to believe they're good in themselves because you are still in that struggle for self-acceptance and you need to say this in order to try to accept yourself."

However, if we find it necessary to refute and deny the gays' feelings before we listen and learn the depth of their hurt, we will not grasp the lesson God wants us to learn. Rather we will find ourselves becoming more frustrated, angry, and thwarted in our attempts to minister.

JOBS

How significant is your job to your own identity, to the well-being of your family? Have you ever been fired? Do you remember how you felt?

As a pastor I have been through the abyss of joblessness with many persons. Some of them were very strong and successful people until their work was terminated. I saw how they needed their spouses, friends, and brothers and sisters in the faith. It rocked the foundation of their self-image.

Lewis Williams says quite well in his article, "Walls of Ice—Theology and Social Policy":

> While American society, including the churches, is now showing a concern about job discrimination against Negroes, the Indians, and the Mexican-Americans, it still actively supports discrimination against the homosexual. If he is a churchman, it says, "You are a sinner; get out." If he is a member of the legal profession, it says, "You are a felon; get out." If he is a teacher, it says, "You are a seducer of the young; get out." If he works for the civil service, it says, "You are an immoral person and a menace to your fellow employees; get out." If he is a serviceman or officer, no matter how distinguished, it says, "You are a threat to discipline and morale; get out" (and attaches a life-long stigma in the form of a less-than-honorable discharge) . . . [7]

This is a very difficult area for us to deal with because such concerns are valid. What rights are improperly being denied? On the other hand, what place should a practicing homosexual ever have as a teacher of our children? Answers need to be found.

Here again, I plead: Please do not let issues keep you from hearing what is being said. We need to understand the gays' struggle in their relationship to jobs. Many of these persons have had to stay in the closet. They know either from their own personal experience or from the experience of others that if they let it be known that they are practicing homosexuals, they will lose their jobs. If that is not the case, at least they lose the likelihood of further advancement. This job threat produces inconceivable fear of detection, and keeps the closet door closed for most homosexuals.

WEEPING WITH THOSE WHO WEEP

I have a friend with whom I have shared many experiences. He is a Christian brother in the process of winning victory over the besetting sin of homosexual practice. He does not fail often. In fact, it's very seldom now.

For my friend, the poem *Please Hear What I'm Saying* has a radically different meaning. He not only has worn masks like we do, but he has had to be extremely careful to have the right mask on at the right time. And while his outward life and his inner life have become more unified, for nearly thirty years there was a giant chasm between the two.

He wanted to be known and yet he was afraid. So he wondered if anybody really loved him. And like most people, he stayed too long in the closet.

You should see what a little kindness and gentleness can do. I saw new life breathed into him. I know how important another Christian brother is to him—that willingness to drop everything else and take whatever time is necessary to get together. We *can* choose to be life and grace to each other.

Please try to understand the pain. Before you judge him, walk a mile in his moccasins. Sit where he sits in the daily struggles of life so that you will learn to "weep with those who weep."

My challenge to the church—and to the gay community—is to " . . . go, and sin no more" (John 8:11, KJV). I cry out for healing and change for the homosexual. It is that concern, that compassion (some say fanaticism) that demands I call homosexual acts sin. It is not in repulsion or rejection or fear. If I see my brother in need and say to him "go and be warm and be fed" without recognizing that the church must help feed and clothe him, then I am *not* loving.

The church has in the past seen the homosexual as a person to hate and reject rather than someone to comfort and heal. The homosexual has been seen as someone to strip the few remaining rags of clothes from rather than to clothe; as someone to starve even more rather than someone to feed.

The time is now, church and fellow Christians, to put these sins behind us. The challenge is clear and open. Thousands of gays are knocking on our doors saying "either heal me or let me have peace with my condition. But for the sake of God and man, do not torture me by condemning me and then refusing to give me the kind of assistance I must have to escape this dilemma."

Church, are you there?

III.

A Time for Hope

10

Hope for the Homosexual

THERE IS NO HOPE for the homosexual if the church of Jesus Christ changes its historical-biblical view of sexuality, morality, homosexuality as sin, or of the necessity to turn from that sin. If Christendom recants, the church will have "gained the whole world, but lost its soul." It would no longer have any authority in Scripture, it would cease following its Lord, Jesus Christ. It may feel somewhat better about itself for a time, but it would have provided only bogus grace, which is no grace at all.

For God justifies the sinner, not the sin.

THE BAD NEWS

The good news for homosexuals begins with the bad news. Homosexuality is contrary to God's nature, which is holy. We have learned it is contrary to His purpose in creation. It is contrary to His plan for life, a fact that led to the destruction of Sodom and Gomorrah. It is contrary to His Law revealed through Moses. It is a perversion of God's intention and is not made right by the appeal to inversion, that is, to being a constitutional homosexual. It is not supportive of family life and the fidelity that Jesus so strongly emphasized. It does not lead to stronger moral character, but involves its victims in all kinds of deceit, manipulation, and lustful behavior.

111

God loves you, but He hates your sin because—
  it is destructive of your well-being;
  it has become an idol in your life;
  it enslaves you instead of setting you free;
  it is clearly contrary to His nature;
  it alienates you from Him and from His people;
  it robs you from establishing lasting relationships;
  it affects your emotional and psychological well-being; and
  it makes you susceptible to all kinds of temptations.
God hates the sin because He loves you, because you are of infinite worth, and because His plan for your life is limited by and misdirected by your sin.

If you are a practicing homosexual, you are in great danger, perilous danger, of being the source of a stumbling block to someone else, especially some younger person. You may lead them into your sexual acts, reinforce their present yearnings, and thereby dress this sin in the guise of respectability. And Jesus said taking a swim with a millstone around your neck would be the easy way out. That is not His desire nor our desire.

The gay lifestyle is not only sinful, but it is also evidence of God's judgment against idolatry—worshiping other creatures rather than the Creator. The Scriptures tell us that God allows homosexuals the "freedom" of doing what they want (see Rom. 1:18–28). This divine denunciation of homosexual sin is enlarged in the *total fabric of Scripture* concerning God's nature: holy, righteous, just, loving, gracious, and forgiving.

> . . . God is light and in him is no darkness at all. If we say we have fellowship with him while we walk in darkness, we lie and do not live according to the truth (1 John 1:5,6).

But this law is given to bring us to Christ—to His grace. The law reveals the immeasurable gap between God and people. No one escapes the staggering dimensions of personal sin.

As I write to you who now think of yourselves as homosexuals, there is no sense within me that I am less sinful than you. I know that I am not. The Scriptures do not allow me that luxury. But I am not seeking to have anyone tell me my sins are okay. In fact, I am deeply grateful that my spiritual mentors had the courage and wisdom not to allow me to soft-soap my transgressions.

You are no more sinful than others, but you need to repent of your sins, all of them, as do all of us. Apart from repentance, there is no forgiveness. This does not mean that you are forgiven because you repent. Repentance is not a good work. It means that *because* you have experienced grace and forgiveness, you want to repent and do repent.

THE GOOD NEWS

God is not only holy, He is also love (see 1 John 4:8). This is the Good News. His nature includes liberating love. He loves you as much as He loves any other living person—including His Son! His love is unconditional. His love is not turned away by our sins; it is only turned away by our wills.

You can receive Him or you can reject Him, but you cannot make His a different kind of love. You cannot come to God on your terms. You cannot put Him or His will into your mold. His love changes people. The more you receive that love, the more He liberates you.

His love does not wink at our sin; He takes it more seriously than we do. He dealt with our sin through Jesus Christ's sacrifice at the Cross. "Behold, the Lamb of God, who takes away the sin of the world!" (John 1:29).

Peter describes it this way:

He himself bore our sins in his body on the tree, that we might *die to sin* and live to righteousness. By his wounds you have been healed. For you were straying like sheep, but have now returned to the Shepherd and Guardian of your souls (1 Pet. 2:24,25, emphasis mine).

Jesus' love for the Father and for us led Him to that Cross.

I am the good shepherd; I know my own and my own know me, as the Father knows me and I know the Father; and I lay down my life for the sheep. . . . No one takes it from me, but I lay it down of my own accord (John 10:14,15,18).

Shortly before His death, Jesus said:

Greater love has no man than this, that a man lay down his life for his friends (John 15:13).

The prodigal son said, "Father, I have sinned against heaven and before you; I am no longer worthy to be called your son" (Luke 15:21). The father didn't even wait for an explanation. He called for the servants: "Get the robe, the best robe. Put the ring of authority on his hand. Put shoes on his feet. Get everything ready for the party. We must have a party. My son is back. My son is back" (Luke 15:22–24, paraphrased).

Please, do come to the party. It's for you. No matter what your sin is, no matter what the past has been, God wipes the slate clean. He has a robe for you—the perfect righteousness of Jesus Christ. It is a gift. The price has already been paid. It is offered totally out of grace. No one even need be worthy—only *willing*.

The Good News includes Jesus' promise of His Holy Spirit. He has promised "rivers of living water" (John 7:38). Not just a trickle, or a stream, but rivers— more than enough. The Comforter, the Spirit of Truth, the Counselor, will come and live in your heart.

The Good News is that God invites you to come just as you are and promises to send you back into the world a changed person. There is hope for the homosexual because God never commands us to do anything without also offering to us the power and strength by which to obey.

Listen to the story of one who is different:

Mine is not the story of a person who had doubts about her sexuality from puberty on. I was always just a normal girl with normal interests. My first year of college I was on my own for the first time and I loved it. I was 19 at the time and I began to develop a relationship with a woman who was 28. I began to suspect my new friend was a lesbian and one night I confronted her. She admitted she was and I began what I thought was to be my great contribution to the human race—I was going to help her overcome this problem.

Our friendship grew, but she began to make it clear that she was not interested in going "straight" and that I need not waste my time. She was happy being gay. During this time I could find no support for my theory that being gay was wrong and being straight was right. Psychology professors taught that different expressions of sexuality were fine, as long as no one was being hurt. The theme of the day was "Do your own thing."

I even went to the university staff psychiatrist for help with my own feelings about the situation. I only remember leaving his office feeling silly for being afraid of becoming gay myself. Everywhere I turned there was approval, or at least lack of concern, over the homosexual. I began to evaluate my own thoughts.

Perhaps *I* was the one with the problem. Why should I try to change someone who is happy? I rationalized that a loving God could not condemn love between two people. What difference could it make if they were the same sex? If two people loved each other and wanted to give their bodies in an act of commitment, trust, and love, could this be condemned?

I had solved *my* problem.

Now I was free to return the love this woman had for me. She had not forced me into anything, for she had made her true feelings known to me only at my insistence. No one had ever demonstrated faith and confidence in me as she had. No one had sought to understand me as she had.

My emotions have always been a big part of my life. She understood this and handled my ups and downs with great loving skill. After all, I reasoned, who could better understand a woman than another woman? No man I had ever met (including relatives) had ever shown understanding and compassion for a woman. From all I had seen, men only thought of themselves. Women were objects of sex alone. I decided to return the love of this woman who loved me. I would not bother myself searching for the nonexistent "perfect man."

We made our commitment and considered ourselves married, beginning what was to be our nine months together. Thus began my new way of life, filled with deceit, caution, hiding, and frustration. Mild tranquilizers calmed my nervous stomach, but I was still unable to eat properly. Between my diet and my constant worry, I lost weight. Despite all of this, I believed I was happy. Society's misguided rejection of the homosexual was the cause of whatever problems I had.

We were separated during summer vacation. I thought this would be more than I could stand. She had become my world, my reason for living, my god. I feared my parents would discover my secret; I was scared to the point of exhaustion.

Then my nightmare came true, they discovered all about my friend. They had me removed from the University and would not allow us to communicate with one another. They promised they would take legal action against my friend for contributing to the delinquency of a minor if we had any further contact. It was hell. The person I loved was being stripped out of my life. They gave me the choice of talking to a psychiatrist or a minister. I chose the minister.

When I arrived at Jerry Kirk's office, I must have been a sight. I weighed 85 pounds, jumped three feet if someone dropped a pencil, and had no concern for my appearance. Jerry could see my spirit was broken and spoke with great compassion and love. He did not read Scriptures, condemning my homosexuality, he simply looked at me and said, "You know you're wrong."

He had hit at the heart of my problem; I did know I was wrong. I found that those standards I had sought while at college did exist, and God did not approve of homosexuality. I conceded the fight, gave my life back to Christ, and began my long, lonely struggle toward change.

Christ was now in my life, but Satan still had a strong foothold. He used every weapon at hand. Everything reminded me of her. My sexual desires seemed uncontrollable at times. I had doubts, and even considered that Jerry had lied to me. I tried to end my life. I wanted desperately to be sure of the real truth. It was eight hard months before I felt a real victory over the temptations of homosexuality.

I married two years after this ordeal to a man truly chosen by the Lord for me. During our first year of marriage I found there were still scars in need of repair by the Lord. Building a marriage is a real struggle for two very normal people, but when one partner brings scar tissue from past relationships, it is twice as hard to stick with it rather than run.

I praise the Lord for His love and concern for my life. I praise His name for Christians like Jerry who showed me a life and a God with conviction and truth. I praise His name for parents not willing to concede or give up on a child gone wrong.

I pray for all those like me who have been led astray by the world. I pray they will always be able to turn to Christians, to see the real truth and find stability in faith. Most of all I pray they find the healing forgiveness and love of Jesus Christ for their lives.

Do you believe there is hope for the homosexual? I say emphatically yes! You see, Jesus Christ was employed on this earth as a carpenter. That was His trade. I imagine that often His mother Mary would bring Him a broken object and ask, "Jesus, would you fix it?" Today, we bring our lives to Him and say, "Please, Lord, fix it." In that sense, He is still a carpenter.

Let me share with you one other changed life.

I was the second of four children raised in a very strict Roman Catholic family. (Both of my sisters are now married and my older brother is presently an avowed homosexual.) Having had a Catholic education all through my schooling, I was deeply rooted in the faith.

My attractions were definitely heterosexual as I was growing up. I experienced a very active dating life. After high school I attended a two-year training program for medical technicians.

In 1968, at the age of 24, I was engaged to be married. After a short period of time, I broke the engagement. Later that same year I met Roberta. We were both employed as medical technicians at a hospital in the West.

For several years now I had begun to question my Catholic faith. Gradually I began to break away. I was desperately searching for some spiritual meaning in my life.

In May of 1969 my roommate was making a move to Florida and I was looking for someone to replace her. Roberta was thrilled that I asked her. I knew she was wanting to move out of her parents' home. Within that year we had become close friends. I had no conception at that time of ever becoming involved with her. Shortly after she moved in, our homosexual relationship began. This was the start of a five-year relationship.

Prior to Roberta moving in with me, I had been dating a young man with whom I was very seriously contemplating marriage. I was brokenhearted and crushed when he suddenly broke up with me. I'm not trying to minimize my blame for my involvement with Roberta, but just stating a fact. I was very hurt and a bit depressed.

My entry into this relationship was accompanied by some guilt feelings. I kept overshadowing them with excuses that homosexual acts were not sinful. I continued to suppress the guilt feelings throughout the remainder of the five years.

As the first few months passed, I realized that Roberta's

entry into this relationship was on an entirely different basis than mine. My reason was solely one of sexual satisfaction. It was at this point that I began to feel trapped. I was beginning to date again, not realizing what Roberta's reaction would be. She immediately displayed anger toward me. I followed with verbal attempts to let her know that my feelings for her were not the same as hers for me. I told her I never intended for anything to develop like this.

Physical fights began to take place. She would make threats to take her own life. A few times those threats turned into actual attempts. I don't know how far she would have really gone, but at that time I felt very sure that she would kill herself if I didn't stop her. I began to play a double role. I would tell her of my true feelings about her, and then I'd end up lying to her and telling her that I really did love her. That's all she wanted to hear. She desperately needed that reassurance. I couldn't stand to hurt her, so over the years I became very soft-hearted. Besides worrying about the physical damage she might cause herself, I was also concerned and afraid of what she would do to me.

I was depressed much of the five years. I was in a situation where I enjoyed and wanted what pleasures I got sexually, but I definitely wanted no part of the additional things Roberta wanted attached to our relationship. She wanted to possess me totally. We would have terrible scenes over my becoming friends with anyone—male or female. She became extremely jealous of even my family.

We could count on very few days to be free of argument. But, foolishly, we would always agree that those few good days outweighed all of the bad ones. Then we would completely contradict ourselves when we faced reality. We would admit at times that what was going on was not right, but saw no hope of getting ourselves out of the pit we'd put ourselves into.

I used to say, "I fell into that pit," but that was only to make myself look good. I could blame no one for letting me fall into that pit. Much of my healing up until this present day has been dealing with that particular thing.

I could have walked out on Roberta any time, but my fear kept me there. Plus I just couldn't hurt her. As the months went by, many bad feelings developed and grew in intensity: hate, self-hate, resentment, bitterness, anger, possessiveness, jealousy, fear, and depression.

Early 1971 found us making plans to move to Cincinnati. We thought a change of scenery would probably make a difference in our lives. We both had acquired jobs as medical technicians in separate doctors' offices.

Things didn't improve. It was as if our lives had become tumbleweeds in a vast never-ending wind. At times the wind might die down a bit, but never enough to keep the weeds from gathering the filth of the earth. Despair had been added to the list.

I had chances to date, but to no avail. The same old "torture cycle" would begin again. During these five years I kept praying for the Lord to rescue us from this mess, but I was not willing to do my part.

In March of 1974, Roberta and I were both introduced to College Hill Presbyterian Church by Pat Robinson. Later that year we joined a small women's prayer group led by Sibyl Towner. The Lord truly began working in our lives. A year and a half passed. However, nothing was actually changing in our relationship toward each other.

December of 1975 marked a crucial point for us. We had one of our worst fights when I accepted a date. We were both in such a fit of anger that we could have easily killed each other. Roberta began shouting, "Let's call someone from the prayer group." We called Sybil.

The next morning she arranged an appointment with Gary Sweeten. That day was the start of some heavy counseling with Gary, and later on with Paul Thierry. Roberta had mixed feelings about seeing him. She didn't want to lose me and yet she knew that sooner or later I wouldn't be around for her to lose. We had taken the big step and called out for help. I knew the Lord was answering my prayer, and I wasn't going to turn my back.

That first day in Gary's office, we both renounced the sin of homosexuality. We had the laying on of hands for healing. What occurred was a miracle. To God be the Glory! There had been several people that the Lord had used as instruments in our lives and Gary was one.

December 17, 1975, marked the first day of victory for the Lord in our lives. Our sexual relationship came to an abrupt halt. Roberta's struggle was a bit harder in that respect—impossible without the Lord!

The days, weeks, and months that followed were very painful. The healings that were taking place in our lives proved to be very difficult, but Jesus was always there to soften the hurt. The healing process has been continuous during these two years.

Although we were *immediately* healed from homosexuality, the resulting factors of that life are still being dealt with by the Lord. There was much pain and heartache. But along with the pain there is that *hope*. Our strength is no longer in ourselves, but in the Lord.

His grace has been made sufficient for us and His power has been made perfect in our weakness. (2 Cor. 12:9.)

Years ago, the hymnwriter Charles Wesley penned, "He breaks the power of cancelled sin; He sets the prisoner free."[1] The hope for the homosexual is in the person of Jesus Christ, and being under the care of His kingdom. As you finish reading this chapter, if you have never done so before, why not:

Turn from your sins.
Ask Jesus Christ to forgive you.
Ask Him to enter your heart and life.
Ask Him to heal you.

These are the first and all important steps to wholeness. Then ask Him to lead you to a fellowship of believers with whom you can become real and through whom you can become whole.

11

Hope for the Homophobiac

BEFORE YOU PICKED up this book, you may not have known that homophobia—the fear and rejection of homosexuals as people—was sin. This may be an entirely new thought to you, but this sin, too, must be dealt with.

It is similar to a counseling situation I might have with a married couple. Let's say the husband has committed adultery and the wife, of course, is expecting me to come down hard on him. She is shocked when I begin to explore her sin. She says, "What? You're blaming *his* sin on *me?*"

No, I am not interested in laying blame. He is responsible for his sin, but this doesn't eliminate her responsibility in the matter. I have to help the wife see that her lack of affection was part of what helped make her husband vulnerable to the tenderness and love of another woman. It's not that her sin is worse, but it was part of the picture.

Likewise, the homosexual has sinned. But Christian, your sin of lovelessness may be keeping him from finding hope and Christ. He may not as yet have found a Christian who will love him as he is and then guide him to wholeness in Christ.

At this point you may be saying, "Come off it, Jerry! You don't understand me. Why, I've *seen* these things! You've been speaking to so many people and reading so many books that your head is in the clouds. You are out of touch."

I don't believe you are any more closed than I was when I began. Are you open to allowing God's Spirit to speak to *you*? Even if you are not, as Sam Shoemaker once said, "Are you open to the possibility of becoming open?"

MY OWN STRUGGLE

My own homophobia is being healed by a slow, gentle process. Part of the reason I believe that much of my homophobia is gone is because gays sense they can come to see me and that my love is not conditional. They end up sending their friends to me. Perhaps it should be said at this point that I am not a homosexual and have never entered into a homosexual experience. They come to me not because I might be a cured homosexual, but because they know that I am a heterosexual who can love them and call them to repentance, forgiveness, and the healing of Christ.

But this has not always been the case. There was a time when I was (perhaps like you) repulsed, shocked, and fearful of a homosexual person.

It was when I was twelve years old that I encountered a homosexual for the first time. I had no idea what was going on. I was in a movie theater in Seattle and the fellow in the next seat put his hand on my knee. I waited a moment, assuming it was an accident and that he would remove it. Surprisingly, he didn't. Finally, I grabbed his hand with all my strength and literally threw it back at him. My adrenalin was pumping full steam. I bolted out of my seat, stalked back up the aisle several rows, and sat down. I stared at the back of that guy's head during much of the movie.

Then, when I was older, I was in a car with a young man who put his arm around my shoulder. I think I was more frightened than anything else because he was in control of the car. It was a legitimate fear of the unknown that made me shout, "Stop this car! I'm getting out of here!"

I know your fear. I also know you can be healed because I have received considerable healing and am still in the process of being healed.

HOW DID YOU GET FROM THERE TO HERE?

For me the healing of my homophobia began when a young man I'll call "Fred" walked into my office. I shared the message of God's love for him and saw him come to the Lord. Months went by and we spent many hours talking and going places together.

Then as I came to know him well, he began to pour out his heart to me. He revealed the struggle that he had had with his father, an experience of almost total rejection. "Jerry," he said, "I can never remember my father showing me any affection or verbally giving me any affirmation. And how I longed for it."

But Fred had experienced the love of God touching him. He was overwhelmed by the realization that God could forgive all and even heal the memories. After he had gained confidence in me and was convinced of my loyalty and trustfulness, he shared with me that he was a homosexual.

If I hadn't known him so well and loved him so much, I might have been repulsed, but our friendship wasn't marred by this new revelation. I knew him and loved him unconditionally, and I didn't stop loving. His knowing this was the biggest thing in his life, and I knew the joy of loving the sinner while hating the sin. I had begun to be healed.

HOMOPHOBIA AND THE GAY MOVEMENT

But beyond the personal realm, there is another dimension to homophobia. It's the natural repulsion and fear we feel against the gay movement. It is not primarily directed against a person, but it can become confused and directed toward an individual who becomes for us symbolic of the gay movement.

We are pushed on all sides by the movement. Our world is being invaded by those who are forcing us to accept open homosexuality and call it good. We become angry and defensive. We find ourselves falling back into the sin of homophobia, especially when we feel militant homosexuals are attacking our sources of security. We want to strike out in defense against them.

My homophobiac sin surfaced when our General Assembly asked us to consider the question of whether an avowed, practicing homosexual could be ordained into the gospel ministry. I was appalled! Our session sent a formal recommendation to the presbytery to request the General Assembly to answer the question once and for all, and to clarify for the New York Presbytery that homosexual acts *are* sinful and contrary to the divine intention and that an avowed, practicing homosexual ought *not* to be ordained to the Presbyterian ministry. The New York Presbytery was asking for "definitive guidance," and we believed it ought to be given, and that right early!

The local presbytery acted favorably on our recommendation, and I was asked to represent them before the assembly committee since I was going to be present at the meeting in Baltimore.

That experience before the committee in public hearings and deliberations was one I'll never forget. If anything could have heightened homophobia, that was it! It made me angry, frustrated, and alienated from my colleagues. The meeting was inundated with gays and gay sympathizers. I began to speak out for the biblical view of sexuality. For the first time in my life I sensed what it was like to be "the leper."

When I had finished, I went out into the hall and said to some of my fellow pastors, "How can you sit there and let this happen? How can you be quiet? For every one or two of us who speak in there, there are five to ten gays and sympathizers speaking out as if this is the wave of the future. You made me feel like an outcast in there, even though I was standing up for what was right."

This began a root of bitterness within me that was not healed until recently. In a worship service with some Jesuit brothers at their renewal center in Cincinnati, the Lord revealed to me the anger I had suppressed for two years. I had prayed about it and then determined not to tell it to others. As we read in the worship service the Old Testament passage about David being harrassed by Absalom, the Lord revealed my anger to me and helped me let go of it.

The next night in the worship service we prayed the Lord's Prayer. Now, the Jesuit brothers use the word *trespasses* and I am accustomed to the word *debts.* "Trespasses" stood out like fire before me. "Forgive us our trespasses, as we forgive those who trespass against us."

I realized then that even though I had let go of the anger the night before, I had never forgiven those people. I said, "Lord, I want to forgive them. I ask you to give me the grace to forgive them." And I *willed* to forgive them. Then I prayed for each one on that committee whom I knew by name, and for the first time in two years I had genuine love for them. I confess to you the memories are not all gone, but I have no sense of the anger. In other words, I need to keep praying for them, that God's love would sweep through the very depths of my being.

I called my wife, Patty, on the phone and said, "Honey, something special has happened. I came here with unresolved anger, but God has met me and healed me." I could not be writing as I am if God had not removed the hurt and anger—and even bitterness. These things were tremendous blocks to my being willing to see my homophobia, let alone wanting to deal with it.

But God is gracious and persistent, and I am thankful for these experiences because love is something you do and not something you feel. If love does not change behavior, or at least initiate the desire for change, it is worse than nothing. It is a noisy gong or a clanging cymbal.

WHY WE FEAR

Why do we have unloving thoughts about homosexuals and sometimes do not even want to be healed? Let's just list some reasons why people feel as they do:

1. Because of bad experiences as children when they were approached by a homosexual.
2. Some were led into a homosexual experience as a child or youth, and it was a very distasteful experience. There was guilt and fear when they found they could not share it with anyone.
3. There may have been a homosexual involvement with someone for a period of time and it seemed good because it seemed loving. Then the roof fell in.
4. Some persons fear that they might be homosexuals, or that they may have tendencies that way, or that they might suddenly fall into it.
5. Some have had loved ones involved, and they have seen the terrible pain.
6. With some repression sets in because of fear and anger, and things get worse when we don't want to talk about them.

We must grant that all these feelings are real and communicated, but there is one more factor. There is proper anger, not against homosexuals, but against *homosexual acts*. There is proper anger against evil as evidenced by our Lord (see Matt. 21:12ff, and Mark 3:5ff).

There are those who believe God has spoken. He is holy and has defined or put limits or frames around the picture of holiness. God's law is truth and the church reflects in many ways what the Scriptures teach about homosexuals. It better! If it doesn't, it's unfaithful to Scripture. This and other biblical truths have not always been held in love, but they *need* to be held . . . and in *love*.

LOVING GOD'S WAY

Jesus said, "[I] must work the works of him who sent me . . ." (John 9:4). How did Jesus work out God's love?

First of all, *He loved people where they were.* He didn't say, "I'll love you if you're good. I'll love you if you measure up. I'll love you if you're worthy." No, He loved the unlovable, and for many this may be the homosexual. His love was unconditional.

You may feel that the homosexual is not worthy of your love. Ask God to forgive you for this and He will if you mean it. Ask Him to fill you with *His* love. You can't pretend that you love them if you really don't. Jesus' love accepts people. The woman at the well and Zacchaeus met the Master and knew they were accepted. If, even by your body language, the homosexual feels that you are shocked and not accepting, he or she will know they can't trust you.

Secondly, *Jesus' love was costly.* He made Himself available. His life was not His own. He gave Himself, so that meant giving His time. That meant interruptions along the way. That meant late nights and early mornings, and talking with women in the middle of the day, and healing sick folk whom no one else could help.

Thirdly, *Jesus' love was consistent.* His love didn't fluctuate. He was loyal to those He loved, not talking about them to others or cutting them down to make Himself feel good.

Could you be loyal to homosexuals who shared their secrets with you and never talk about them with others? Would your love be consistent? Would they know that if they failed, you would still be there, that you would still care and not give up on them? If they fell, could they get up and start again with God's forgiveness and your short memory? Think of Peter. After his triple play of denial, he knew Jesus had forgiven him.

Fourthly, *Jesus loved by His words and actions.* He was not reticent about confronting evil or selfishness in the apostles or hypocrisy in the Pharisees. That was love too, tough love.

Would you love homosexuals enough to confront their sin, to take them and their sin seriously enough to call them to repentance, forgiveness, and healing? Remember, it's not sloppy agape, it's liberating love.

Many times I say, "Let's hold one another accountable." I call it mutual accountability. The church needs mutual accountability. I tell them about one of my needs and I ask them to pray for me. Then when we come together again I say, "How are you doing?" And I get it right back, "And how are *you* doing?"

We must not become the judge. God is the judge and God alone. He has made that clear. His judgment is just, while ours, at best, is tainted. His judgment is knowledgeable, while ours is limited. This does not mean, however, that we are not to discipline one another.

And then we need to remember that the Judge is also our Saviour (see Rom. 8:32). The Judge went to the cross. He is our Advocate (see 1 John 2:1). The Judge is also the One who calls us to love His way and who says to us and to all sinners, " . . . go, and sin no more" (John 8:11, KJV).

Fifthly, *Jesus' love to sinners was gentle and kind.* He loved them by taking time to listen. He made people feel worthwhile. In his presence people had significance and usefulness.

He taught and He lived as though every person were important, including lepers, women, children, the lame, and the poor. His sense of self-importance did not need to be shored up by the importance of those with whom He ate and traveled.

Would the homosexual see in you the gentleness and kindness of Jesus? Harsh words have tightened the graveclothes around him. Kind words can loose them. I can't say enough about this. Cruel words and jokes hurt these sensitive people so deeply. Their wounds are raw and sore. As you gently remove the rag covering the wound, it might be stuck. And he might scream out in pain, "No, don't. It hurts too much! Don't pull it off." But here's where our love has to be tough. The bandage must come off so the wound can get air and heal. But go slowly, be gentle.

Finally, *Jesus' love was demanding.* He called His followers to take up their crosses daily. He called His disciples to obedience to Him and to the Father (see John 14:21). He called them to God's best in their lives, to moral purity and faith.

There are three keys to helping homosexuals or homophobiacs or other sinners:

1. Make sure they are aware that you know *you* are as big a sinner as they. (And don't fake it. If you don't believe you're as big a sinner, *how come?*)
2. Accept them as friends—real friends.
3. Call them to a godly life.

IV.

A Time for Action

12

How to Effect Change: Mobilization

LET'S KEEP OUR GOALS clear about the unity and the purity of the church. How important to you is the life and unity of your congregation, your denomination, and the total body of Christ? And before you answer that question ask this one as well: How important is unity in the church to Jesus Christ?

In His high priestly prayer Jesus said, "I do not pray for these only, but also for those who believe in me through their word, that they may all be one; even as thou, Father, art in me, and I in thee, that they also may be in us, so that the world may believe that thou hast sent me" (John 17:20, 21).

OUR UNITY

Jesus was praying for the unity of those who were to believe in Him. Unity is a high priority of our Lord, both unity of the church universal and unity of the people in individual congregations. If you are concerned for the unity and well-being of your local parish, should you not also be concerned for the well-being and unity of thousands of similar congregations both small and large? How important are these congregations to Christ? How important are the individuals within them to Him—both heterosexual and homosexual? The unity and love of

God's people for one another must never be far from our thinking, because it is on the heart of our Lord. He has made that clear.

Dr. Richard Halverson is a United Presbyterian pastor in Washington, D.C. In one of his weekly newsletters to businessmen, he writes about a love that cares enough to fight—to fight to preserve the love relationship.

> If you're going to fight . . .
> Fight *for* the relationship—*not against* it!
> Fight *for reconciliation*—not for alienation.
> Fight to *preserve the friendship*—not to
>   destroy it.
>
> Fight to *win your spouse*—not to lose him/her.
> Fight to *save your marriage*—not to cash it in.
> Fight to solve the problem—*not to salve your ego!*
>
> If you're going to fight . . .
> *Fight to win* . . . not to lose!
> Lasting relationships are not negotiated . . . *they are forged.*
>
> That means *heat and pressure.*
> It is *commitment to a relationship* which sustains it . . . not
>   pleasant feelings.
>
> Treat a relationship as negotiable—it is *easily lost.*
>
> Consider it non-negotiable—*a way is found to make it
>   work.*
>
> Authentic intimacy comes *only through struggle.*[1]

OUR PURITY

The purity of the church is also of great importance to Jesus. The homosexual crisis has been precipitated within the church, and we must respond with firmness as well as compassion. God's rights take precedence. His honor and truth and the well-being of His people are at stake.

Prepare yourself by being open and by seeking knowledge. Trust God and not your efforts. Allow the compassion of Christ to grow within you and the cutting edge of Christ's convictions to give you courage. Prepare yourself for "speaking the truth in love" (Eph. 4:15). Then speak up and speak out and let your voice be heard. No one should stand on the fence on this issue. Everyone needs to be heard.

There is great danger in wrong reaction concerning this issue. Many people respond in anger or out of fear. If done in the wrong spirit, writing or speaking against homosexuality as an acceptable lifestyle would do little to preserve church unity and purity. But there is no danger in being too concerned or too well prepared. There is no danger in going to the right people in the right spirit.

> Speak with wisdom
> Speak with love
> Speak with conviction;
>   but not in anger or hate or fear.[2]

THE MATTER OF MOMENTUM

The momentum is not on the side of ordination of practicing homosexuals. These forces have had some gains in recent years, and the impact of the mass media is presently on their side. But let's put that into proper perspective so that we can help effect change and mobilize the people of Christ's church—not out of fear, but out of love; not defensively, but in the confidence that Christ is Lord of this issue.

We have the witness of Scripture in text and context and in biblical theology. We have the major confessions and creeds that speak to the issues of morality and God's law. The great theologians for twenty centuries have been nearly unanimous in their analysis of Scripture, and in their comments upon its teaching about homosexuality. Finally, lest we forget, we have the witness of the Holy Spirit speaking truth to our hearts and minds. The witness is consistent.

Why all the fuss if this is the case? Because in the past eight years the gays have come out of the closet, have found a new identity, have made considerable gains in the medical and psychological field (they would like us to think), and above all have found exposure through the mass media.

But where are they in the church? Gays have established one hundred Metropolitan Community Churches for homosexuals, organized small gay caucuses in most large denominations, and rallied many gay sympathizers among the liberals who have very little commitment to biblical authority.

There have been two avowed homosexuals ordained in mainline denominations, William Johnson by the Golden Gate Association of the United Church of Christ in San Francisco, and Ellen Barrett by Bishop Moore of the Episcopal Church in New York City. Neither of these persons has been called to pastor a church, and strong reaction against their ordination has been evident from within and without those churches.

What about United Presbyterians? In early 1978, the momentum *appears* to be on the side of accepting the gay lifestyle as a valid Christian option and of ordination of practicing homosexuals. That momentum is supplied by fourteen persons on the Homosexuality Task Force and twelve persons on the Advisory Council on Church and Society. The task force itself was appointed by the chairperson of the Advisory Council on Church and Society with help from the moderator of the General Assembly. Those twenty-six persons have provided the momentum and nearly all the leadership has been provided by the Advisory Council on Church and Society. (For a further discussion of this situation, please see the appendix, "For Presbyterians Only"). That momentum is more illusory than real. Add to these twenty-six persons a small group of persons in the New York Presbytery and among our national staff, and a few hundred gays or gay sympathizers in various parts of the country, and you have the foundation of the present momentum—which looks more like a balloon that is about to burst.

Why have I indicated that I believe the momentum is on our side? Because I want you to act, not out of desperation or anger or hate, but out of awareness of the facts. We have every conceivable reason to play as if we were winning in terms of this decision—because we are. Presbytery after presbytery is taking a stand. The Chicago and Detroit presbyteries are among the many. But that doesn't mean we do one thing differently than we would if the situation were almost hopeless.

Be assured that God is sovereign, that His truth is what matters, and that it is His kingdom and His church and His power. We work not just to win the decision, but to learn to love homosexuals and to seek God's blessing for moral strength in our church and our country.

THE BATTLE FOR THE KINGDOM

The battle is not just a decision for or against ordination of homosexuals. The battle is against moral laxity within the life of the church (its clergy and laity) and in our nation. The battle is for more stable and wholesome family life. The battle is for deeper spiritual vitality and for congregational renewal. God is calling the church to a new sense of prophetic clarity in private morality and for pastoral compassion in ministry to broken people.

However, the ordination issue *is* critical in terms of the future well-being of our church and of His church.

WHAT YOU CAN DO—STEP BY STEP

Some people enjoy a sense of freedom from responsibility because they assume they are helpless to change things. Vic Jamieson, in a speech given about six years ago, made this quote from *Harper's* magazine:

> All too often, we prefer to imagine ourselves victims, pathetic insects, caught in the web of technological systems beyond our control . . . maybe a quite different condition prevails. Perhaps we possess too much power, even as individuals, and our powerlessness is a convenient excuse. . . . The truth about technology is not simply that we are small cogs in big machines, but that each cog has remarkable power to effect the machine for good or evil. . . . The *illusion of powerlessness* may yet prove to be the most dangerous by-product of an advanced technology.[3]

You are *not* powerless. God's Spirit is the source of *all* power. Together, we can influence wholesome change in every congregation and denominational structure.

START WHERE YOU ARE

Remember, you are the church. You do not join the church. The church is people, not mortar and not organization. It is the body of believers gathered for worship, study, fellowship, service, and witness. Believers are "salt" to those around them and to those called to serve over them.

You begin your influence among the people with whom God has naturally knit your life. This means family, friends, Sunday school classes, couples groups, and fellowship groups. Visit with neighbors who may belong to your church or some other Christian church. Tell them of your concern and help them become aware of the facts by answering their questions or sharing this book with them.

USE YOUR CONSTITUTIONAL RIGHTS

Leadership is called to serve. Leaders need feedback so they can better reflect the convictions of God's truth and God's people.

The time has come for all concerned Christians to learn how to effect change in and through their particular church in relationship to the homosexual crisis. Political processes are a way to get things done. They can be used either for good purposes or for ill—to build fellowship and trust or to manipulate. I want to speak particularly of the United Presbyterian structure since that is my church and since the deadline is most immediate. I believe others will find these same thoughts helpful for their situations. At this point, it is crucial that you understand the constitution and workings of your local church and the denomination of which you are a member. Once you have this understanding, you can begin to communicate your convictions to those in various levels of leadership.

Communicate With Your Pastor

Talk to your pastor personally about your concerns or write him a sensitive and responsible letter. Say it with love. Encourage other persons to do the same. Be eager to share your thoughts, but also be open to hear his. This is a time for us all to grow. We need not fear knowledge. None of us knows all we need to know about this problem.

Communicate With Your Session (Offical Board)

Write to or talk with members of your session or official board individually. Do so with great care in honor of their heavy responsibilities in this area. Write to your Clerk of

Session in care of your church asking for guidance from the session and requesting information as to what it intends to say and do. Such letters are read in session meetings and given serious attention by elders and pastors.

There is something even more powerful than letters. You and some of your friends may ask to meet with the session and make your convictions known. This is an important way that you can be heard and can effect change on this and other issues. It is especially helpful if other faithful and loving leaders within the church go with you. Prepare carefully and prayerfully—do not hesitate to use your God-given constitutional rights as a United Presbyterian.

We do have a representative form of church government and the voice of the people is very important. (My contacts with persons in other denominations say to me that even the more hierarchical churches are moving much more in the direction of shared leadership, which relies heavily on feedback from lay people. Most ecclesiastical leaders have emerged because they hold in balance deep personal convictions and sensitivity to others.)

Direct Communication to the General Assembly

A special committee is established by the General Assembly to receive all communications dealing with a specific issue. This allows the opportunity for every member to be heard by letter on this issue. Your letters will be read by commissioners to the General Assembly elected to this committee. They should be sent to the Office of the General Assembly, in care of Dr. William P. Thompson, Stated Clerk, 475 Riverside Drive, New York, New York (10027).

Again, may I suggest that you write briefly, responsibly, lovingly, and clearly. Do it out of love for the unity and purity of Christ's church.

Elders, Communicate With the Presbytery (Regional Bodies)

Your session and official boards have tremendous influence in your church structure, especially on those structures immediately above them. Very few people realize how important they are. A single elder can initiate recommendations within the session; that session can initiate proposals that can determine the directions for the presbytery; and ultimately guide the General Assembly. The final outcome is determined by the quality of what you do.

Just as your session takes seriously whatever a member properly writes to them, a presbytery takes very seriously offical communications from sessions. When a session makes an overture (recommendation) to a presbytery, that overture must be presented and acted upon by the entire presbytery. Obviously, that is a time-consuming job and therefore ought to be done with great care. But few issues have ever deserved such action more than the homosexual issue.

Elders, on this issue you are being asked what you believe to be the necessary qualifications for your pastors and the pastors of all Presbyterian congregations. You cannot fulfill your responsibility without speaking out on this issue. However, your greatest responsibility is to your own people, aiding their understanding and giving reassurance. The people want to know where you stand and how deeply you are concerned.

They also need to know if you are knowledgeable and are responding lovingly and firmly, or angrily and defensively. Many of them need your help because they are angry. I have received many letters and comments that I could not repeat in this book. A real part of your ministry is to listen, to absorb hostility, and to help people think about Scripture concerning God's teaching on homosexuality on the one hand, and His call to gentleness, love, and prayer for those who are broken on the other. You are bridge-builders and reconcilers and teachers of God's people. Your spiritual guidance is very much needed at this time.

It is important that sessions study the matter not only now, in preparation for the General Assembly, but also in the months following, so that energies are used to deal constructively rather than defensively with the homosexual issue. This is true in all denominations. Our ministry of love to practicing homosexuals will not happen without study, prayer, and honest sharing of inadequacy and ideas.

Presbytery, Communicate Your Convictions to the General Assembly

Every presbytery should express itself concerning this matter prior to the General Assembly. In the Presbyterian system, primary authority is located in the presbytery. This is the situation historically and practically. Of all the courts of the church, the presbyteries are the most influential and the most responsive to local congregations. Pastors and elders have the best opportunity of expressing themselves and exerting leadership at that level. There is opportunity for mutual accountability between congregations and the presbytery.

So many congregations are deeply disturbed by the majority report that they need to know not only where their session stands, but where their presbytery stands as well. This provides a marvelous opportunity for congregations, and individuals within congregations, to gain confidence in their presbyteries during a time of serious doubt concerning the General Assembly, the Advisory Council on Church and Society, and the task force.

But presbyteries should not stop with speaking out

against ordaining homosexuals. If they do, they will have missed one of the greatest blessings of these two years of study. The minority report stresses that sessions and congregations recognize their failure in ministry to and with practicing homosexuals, and their need to take definite steps toward a ministry of love.

Leaders, Stand Up and Be Counted

It would be helpful both at the presbytery level and at the General Assembly level if people voted on this issue by name. I have often noticed in the past that when a very important issue was before the presbytery or General Assembly many persons wanted their vote recorded. I believe in that. For instance, each member of the task force signed either the majority or the minority report. They did not straddle the fence. I'm sure many, if not all, anguished over their decision. Then, they signed their name to the bottom line.

This was also true of the Advisory Council on Church and Society. They voted twelve to three. They had to decide where they stood. We should do no less.

If congregations knew how their pastors and elders voted at the presbytery, there would be much more dialogue between individuals and their elected representatives. Such dialogue would strengthen our constitutional system. Congregations would not feel so isolated and alienated from the decisions of the presbytery and General Assembly if this were done. I also believe that the outcome of some of the votes would be different. The dialogue would not only influence the lay people in their thoughts, but in some cases the delegates to the presbytery and the commissioners to the General Assembly would also be influenced. There would be more accountability between the commissioners sent to the General Assembly and their presbyteries if their votes were recorded.

LET THE ASSEMBLY SPEAK TO THE CHURCH

The task force has spoken. The Advisory Council on Church and Society has spoken. The people, the sessions, and the presbyteries are speaking. Now the church needs to hear from the General Assembly. The world needs to hear from the church. And the church needs to hear from the Lord.

13

Love That Lasts— A Reconciling Community

> . . . Do not be deceived; neither the immoral, nor idolaters, nor adulterers, nor sexual perverts, nor thieves, nor the greedy, nor drunkards, nor revilers, nor robbers will inherit the Kingdom of God. And such were some of you. But you were washed, you were sanctified, you were justified in the name of the Lord Jesus Christ and in the Spirit of our God.—1 Corinthians 6:9–11

THE EARLY CHURCH was filled with "formers" . . . former habitual sinners who were changed by Christ. The present controversy among Christians is bound to have a positive pay-off in at least one area. Pastors, leaders, and attenders will all be confronted with the disturbing question of whether or not the church continues to transform people from habitually immoral practices to behavior characterized by love, responsibility, and morality based on Christian ethics.

This chapter will set out some helpful directions for church leaders in responding to the real needs of their people. The conclusion of this book is really a beginning. It's a call for Christians to begin to powerfully minister to broken people, to honestly say to the gays, the alcoholics, the depressives, and other hurting, despairing people that Christ's love and power will change their lives.

Frank Worthen of the Love in Action ministry to gays says getting straight is simple. Painfully simple. But it may be the hardest simple thing a homosexual has ever attempted. The three simple steps are:

1. Agree with God that homosexual acts are sinful and are bad for those who practice them. Agree from the heart and the head.

2. Believe that God can change someone—that He has life-changing power available by His Spirit.

3. Submit totally to God's will and His ways.[1]

With those three assumptions we begin the final chapter.

BASIC MARKS OF A RECONCILING CHURCH

The specific marks of a renewed, dynamic, reconciling community of believers are several.[2] First, people are changed only when Scripture is taught and preached as God's word to men and women. People must "renew their minds" in order to be transformed into Christ's image. Secondly, an attempt must be made to implement the principles of Scripture. The Scripture in word and deed provides the basis and power for change.

There are many facets to living out the gospel. The following items will focus on those facets most closely related to the church that will provide means of grace and sanctification to its people.

Evangelism

A must for renewal is an active evangelism program in which persons are consistently experiencing the new

birth of Jesus Christ. Churches without a strong evangelism thrust will die organically and numerically.[3]

Ministry by Clergy and Laity

Our church's approach emphasizes a helper-seeker relationship rather than a counselor-client or therapist-
patient approach. Since *all* persons are broken in some
way, we need the reconciling, sanctifying movement of
the Holy Spirit to make us into the image of Christ. Thus,
as a pastor sharing with a man struggling with sexual
identity, I am a helper, for he is asking my assistance. The
roles often reverse, however, and I suddenly become a
seeker who needs my brother's aid.

We make a concerted effort to diminish the unscriptural
distinctions that have crept in between "clergy" and
"laity." This is true for many reasons. There are simply
not enough clergy to meet all the needs; many clergy are
not gifted in these areas; it is not the call of pastors to be
gifted primarily in counseling; many lay persons are
gifted; many non-clergy are called to a ministry of helping
and are more effective than clergy *or* professional counselors.[4]

Equipping

A specific program must be designed to equip the professional clergy and members of a congregation in helping
and human relations skills, such as active listening skills,
how to give scriptural counsel, and how to know when to
refer. This may require professionals from the community
or other areas to assist in the training.[5]

Group Support

An extensive, well-planned small-group support system
is necessary throughout the local church. Personal, caring
support is needed for all Christians. There needs to be
specific "growth groups" for broken, hurting people. The

Love in Action ministry has such groups as a central thrust of its work.

The church must be a "healing community" where healing is seen as synonymous with sanctification. At a recent meeting of religious and mental health professionals in Cincinnati, psychiatrist Dr. Marshall Ginsberg noted that approximately 40 percent of all persons seeking emotional or interpersonal assistance approach clergy first. Only 20 percent seek a physician and a very small 6 to 7 percent approach a mental health professional.[6]

Dr. Ginsberg went on to say that quite often the counselor's most difficult problem is sorting out the spiritual from the emotional, and that the church is in the most strategic position to discern people with problems.[7]

In light of these and other similar statements, the church of Jesus Christ needs to become mobilized for ministry to broken people.

Acceptance

An atmosphere of grace rather than works/righteousness will show the church to be a "hospital for sinners" rather than a "select club for the righteous." We must be transparent in our testimonies of struggles and victory; we must have compassion and concern toward hurting people; we must offer hope for substantial healing of all persons—regardless of their difficulty; we must be open to diversity and variety of experiences and styles.

Acceptance—not rejection—is the key point in the healing of broken people. Because of their self-awareness, broken people have an uncanny ability to sense rejection. The Jesus Outreach Center, a ministry to gays and others in West Virginia, sets as its *prime basis* of ministry a *warm, caring acceptance of all persons*. And that point has been repeated by many Christians in helping ministries.

This point cannot be over-emphasized. Too often broken men and women have sensed that they were only welcome in the church if and when they got their "act together." An alcoholic said to me that Alcoholics Anonymous accepted him and then helped him change, but the church said that when he changed they would accept him. What a profound difference.

Read part of a letter from a man in our congregation.

I have known many of you for years, and some of you are dear and close friends; however, you do not know that I am a homosexual. I would very much like to tell you who I am, but I can't believe you could handle it. I have seen hatred among you that I have never seen before. Hatred that is heaped upon sin and sinner alike. It frightens me and it is ugly and it grieves me to see you like this.

I know that the reports and resolutions all state that the homosexual should be loved and to be made to turn away from his sin, but this is such a *shallow statement* that it just doesn't encourage the homosexual to come out of his closet to seek your help. I would like very much to tell you who I am and to confess my sin to you. I cannot tell my mother and father, my brothers and sisters.

If I came to you right now and confessed my sin, would it make any difference in our relationship? Would you continue to accept me as your brother in Christ? Would you *guard* my secret? Could I talk with you without adding to my sense of guilt? Would you pray for me? Could you love me?

Remember, I may be a close friend of many years. Are you sure you could handle it? If your answers to these questions are all "yes" would you please stand? I desperately need you.

Yours in Christ,

A Sinner

Recognition of God's Ability

The church must have a deep commitment to God's ability to meet our needs—a high opinion of God. Prayer, fasting, spiritual warfare, and the power and grace to minister in His name are basic.

Meaningful Worship

Deep, moving, meaningful worship experiences that transform the heart and the intellect are needed. Worship must provide those positive "peak" experiences that psychologists and counselors know are important.

POINTS TO CONSIDER WHEN GIVING HELP

All deeply abiding habitual behaviors, such as homosexuality, alcoholism, and depression, have many factors that underlie the cause. Thus any approach to changing that behavior must usually deal with the whole person and not with just one or two facets of the whole. Some of the facets that may need restoration in the life of a needy person are:

1. *Genetic predisposition.* Although there is little data to support the view that homosexuality may be due to genetic predisposition, prayer for physical change as well as appropriate medicines might be used to overcome this.
2. *Early childhood experiences that wounded the person.* Rejection by parents, a "smothering" parent, and child abuse all contribute to our present situation. Prayer therapy has been used with great success with many persons who need their memories healed.[8]
3. *Defensive maneuvers.* When wounded and hurt, the child seeks ways to protect himself from further wounds. Thus a *decision* is made to use nonproduc-

tive ways to get his needs met. For example, a young man who does not have a father who shows him warmth, affection, and concern, might look to relationships with members of the same sex to get those needs met. The need is met in a *distorted* manner, but one that may *feel* better than proper relationships. This is a self-defeating and inappropriate choice for need fulfillment.

4. *Reinforcement of willful behavior.* This inappropriate choice involves a decision of the *will*. If the behavior is to continue, the *willful* choice must be made over and over again. Thus this strong drive of the will must be broken if the behavior is to cease.

These willful behaviors are strongly connected to the ability to imagine. The power of the mind to imagine, to dream, and to fantasize is a tool for either God or Satan. Satan uses this power to convince people that they are homosexuals. Once convinced, it becomes a self-fulfilling prophecy.

If a young man or woman assumes a different sexual identity, then each experience and imagination that supports that assumption will be "proof" of the validity of the assumption. The inappropriate choice of emotional need fulfillment mentioned above (point 3.) will only continue if the behavior is rewarded in some way.

Adult homosexuals often have many years of thought and/or physical behavior that have been rewarded in one way or another. If this behavior is to change, one must discern what the rewards are and change them. For example, it is not always the sexual relationship that is the reward, but the contact with another male (or female).

The other side of this coin in developmental processes is as important for us to understand. If some behavior is *punished*, that behavior is likely not to continue. If a young boy receives strong mothering and weak fathering, he may develop a desire for male relationships that become sexual in nature. These can be rewarded through both sexual release (a very powerful reinforcer) and satisfying male contact.

At the same time, the sexual desires for his mother may so frighten the person that the fear is transferred to most or all women. Thus, whenever he experiences anxiety or fear of a woman, there is a negative reinforcement present. So one often deals with two or more issues at once. A strong fear of women and a strongly reinforced relationship with men. Habit patterns develop that have a tremendous drive of their own.

5. *Intellectual input.* The knowledge one has affects how he deals with his behavior. Facts that we have learned help determine how we live.

   At the root of one's being are the heart issues— moral and spiritual matters that affect every other area. Christ viewed this area to be key in ministering wholeness to hurting people.

6. *Demonic interference.* Christ knew that quite often the people He met needed deliverance from demonic oppression. When that was apparent He showed that the kingdom of God was present (see Luke 11:20) by commanding those spirits to depart. As *one of the several* areas that demand our involvement, deliverance can give us powerful intervention for bringing wholeness to broken people.

7. *Bitterness.* An important point of this facet is a clear conscience. Very often deeply-wounded people have developed a "root of bitterness" (see Heb. 12:15) against parents or significant others which they have nursed for years. It may be so deep that they even deny its presence. However, without a conscious, willful forgiveness of the sin of others,

one cannot himself experience forgiveness (see Matt. 6:12).

THE RESULTING LIFESTYLE

When one's habits, defense mechanisms, emotional states, behavioral patterns, intellect, and moral and spiritual life focus around one facet of life, then we say that the person has a lifestyle—be it homosexuality, drugs, alcohol, heterosexuality, music, Christianity, or whatever. Many of the persons to whom the church preaches have a lifestyle alien to the standards of the righteousness of Christ. The sanctification process is essentially a moving of Christians out of the kingdom of darkness into the kingdom of Light.

All of us develop lifestyles that are pervasive and incredibly difficult to change. Some have a lifestyle of self-centered pride that shows itself in cool aloofness and disdain; others are divisive; some are gossips. In any event, any change in lifestyle comes slowly and over time. We Christians need to become more expert in helping people conform to the standards of the righteousness of Christ.

Homosexuality is often a lifestyle of complex interaction of the whole person for his entire life. This lifestyle involves self image, dependency needs, behavior, interpersonal relationships, spiritual condition, knowledge, parental models, morality, etc. It also includes specific sex acts. Thus, ministering wholeness requires ministry to the whole person as well as to all the parts.

As Christ affects every aspect of life, so does the helping-counseling process. Many of the ways a Christian helper approaches persons are unique, but then many are the results of common sense. I once heard that the best Christian counselor is a person who has sanctified common sense.

Here are some obvious vehicles to help restore a person with an unacceptable lifestyle to spiritual health:[9]

1. Intercessory prayer for the person in need
2. Sharing of key biblical truths
   a. Grace—Ephesians 1 and 2
   b. Self image—1 Corinthians 13
   c. Emotions we all share—consult a Concordance!
   d. Interpersonal relationships in the Church—Ephesians 5
   e. True and false guilt—1 John 1
   f. Forgiveness—Hebrews 10
3. Praying together
   a. Minister to one another
   b. Pray for others
4. Supernatural experiences for the seeker
   a. Being born again
   b. Being filled with the Spirit
   c. Confession, repentance, restoration
5. Miraculous intervention
   a. Physical healing
   b. Inner healing
   c. Deliverance
6. Sharing Christian testimony
   a. Helper shares his own faith
   b. Books, tapes, articles
7. Facilitating awareness of God
   a. Prayer
   b. Fasting
   c. Christian meditation
   d. Renewing the mind—Scripture
8. Worship
   a. Sacraments
   b. Praise
   c. Singing
9. A unified system of truth: standards of normalcy, ethics, and morality

  a. All things work together for good—Romans 8:28
  b. Eternal salvation—John 10:27–30
  c. The love of God—John 3:16–18
  d. Relationships—Colossians 2
 10. Deep supportive Christian fellowship in both large and small gatherings of the church.

THE "HELPER"

The most effective helper is one who uses all that he or she is to minister fully to all that the seeker is.
Let me list a few specifics:

1. At times a helper must confront, share genuine feelings, point out concrete, specific pitfalls, and hold the seeker accountable for his behavior. Nonjudgmental acceptance and sincere confrontation are required at various times in the life span of establishing a relationship with Christ and His people.

    In dealing with deeply broken persons, total honesty, confrontation, and accountability are indispensable. The defense mechanisms developed to cover up fear of detection and then rejection may grow before they subside. The helper must love the seeker enough to probe into those areas that may surface out of confrontation and accountability.

2. Total *acceptance* and *respect* for the dignity of the seeker are critical. But that acceptance and dignity are only truly shown when the helper is willing to risk speaking the truth in love. Otherwise acceptance is based on denying truth, which shows that the helper does not respect the seeker enough to level with him. This kind of conditional acceptance and conditional respect are less than what a helping relationship requires.

3. Give specific direction as it is appropriate. It is also true that the Christian helper will desire *at times* to

teach, to pray, to covenant, to worship. However, there are also times that he or she will listen, reinforce positive behavior, or refer the seeker to a physician for medicine. Beware of simplistic answers to complex questions. And beware of persons, Christian or not, who would fail to minister to the whole person by applying the helping relationship to only *part* of a person's experiences.

4. Walk by faith. Point three above does not mean to say that persons with a simple approach cannot be helpful to broken people. God can use people whose only response to a problem is to say "God calls us to give thanks in all circumstances" or to teach the Scripture. I know He can and will use the person who is untrained but available. Some of the most dramatic changes I have ever seen in persons have resulted from little more than a person who cared, was committed to stick it out with the seeker, and prayed faithfully and vigorously. In the final analysis, there is no more beautiful model than that of people who care, who stay with the one in pain, who pray long and hard, and trust in God rather than in themselves.

5. Establish a secure relationship with the seeker. Brokenness occurs in the context of relationships, thus healing must come in the same way. Where there has been rejection, now there must be Christian acceptance. Where there has been unconcern, let there now be support and interest. Where there has been unhealthy, manipulative, and self-defeating relationships, let us speak the truth in love and be open and honest. There must be this emotional and relational renurturing for broken people.

LOOKING BACK

Perhaps God has brought the spectre of gay ordination to the churches because He was tired of platitudes and cheap talk. Maybe He knew that this is an issue that won't go away and cannot be changed without the "fervent prayer of righteous persons" (see James 5:16). Our anger, our fear, our resentment, our petty words, our cries of Lord! Lord! will not work. Only a commitment of our total selves to Jesus the Christ and to His work will meet the needs of the gay Christian. . . And the frigid Christian, the impotent Christian, the angry Christian, the gossipy Christian, the materialistic Christian, the preachy Christian, the divisive Christian, the hateful Christian, the rejecting Christian.

What is your church going to do differently to minister to the broken hearted? What, my brother and sister, are you going to do differently? As the Holy Spirit prompts you, make a specific commitment *now* to be available to Jesus Christ in fresh and creative ways. Ask for a specific person who is caught in homosexuality to whom you can bear witness in word and deed, and with whom you can be *love that lasts.* But don't do it alone. Find some caring brothers and sisters with whom you can do it. Then you will be part of a reconciling community.*

---

*For additional resource material on congregational renewal, see page 192 of this volume.

Appendix 1.
For Presbyterians Only

THESIS I

THE COUNCIL on Church and Society, predecessor to the present Advisory Council on Church and Society, sought to lead the United Presbyterian Church to redefine the biblical view of sexuality as it relates to premarital and extramarital sex and to homosexual acts. That goal has continued since 1966. Only the senior staff person of the original council serves to the present.

Supporting Data

1. The Council on Church and Society *appointed* a task force in 1966 to study and report to the General Assembly on sexuality.
2. That report entitled "Sexuality and the Human Community" was presented to the 182nd General Assembly in 1970 through the leadership of the Council.
3. That report aimed to open the door:
   a. to premarital sex as a viable Christian expression[1]
   b. to extramarital sex[2]
   c. to homosexual relationships[3]

It was in response to that report and because of disagreement with its conclusions that the Assembly did not direct or initiate a denomination-wide study of the report in the presbyteries and congregations.

The 182nd General Assembly (1970):

> Receives the report "Sexuality and the Human Community," for study; this action is not to be construed as an endorsement of the report.[4]

It was in basic contradiction of the contents of that report that the Assembly continued to act and say,

1. We, the 182nd General Assembly (1970), reaffirm our adherence to the moral law of God as revealed in the Old and New Testament that adultery, prostitution, fornication, and/or the practice of homosexuality is sin. We further affirm our belief in the extension Jesus gave to the law, that the attitude of lust in a man's heart is likewise sin. Also we affirm that any self-righteous attitude of others who would condemn persons who have so sinned is also sin.[5]

2. We require that this statement be included in any publication of this document.[6]

That report on sexuality did not come out of a vacuum. It came from leadership by the Council on Church and Society.

I do not know whether another study on sexuality with similar goals is being considered at the present time, but that is a very strong possibility.

THESIS II

The Advisory Council on Church and Society worked diligently and improperly if not injudiciously to bring about a study on homosexuality and *to see to it that the study would be carried out under its leadership*. It is presently forcefully seeking to influence the church to affirm homosexual acts as good and to recommend that persons who practice them should be ordained. This does not seem to be its proper constitutional role in the church as an advisory council.

Areas of Concern

1. Relationship between New York Presbytery's overture and the Advisory Council on Church and Society.

2. A "Prospectus for a Study of Homosexuality" and the Advice and Counsel Memorandum and the way these documents were used in the Bills and Overtures Committee, 1976.

3. Personal involvement within the Bills and Overtures Committee by members and staff of the Advisory Council on Church and Society.

4. The appointment of the General Assembly Task Force on Homosexuality and its continuing relationship to the Advisory Council on Church and Society.

Supporting Data

1. The relationship between New York Presbytery's overture and the Advisory Council on Church and Society's action to prepare their "Prospectus" was at least similar in timing and location.

   a. New York Presbytery overtured the Assembly on November 11, 1975, and communicated that to the Clerk on December 16th. That overture said:

   The Presbytery of New York City does not find *sufficient guidance* in the Constitution for a person who is an avowed homosexual and is well qualified in every other part of trials for ordination.

   Since a person is ordained for the *whole Church* and the *General Assembly is the final authority* on matters of doctrine and the interpretation of the Constitution of the Church;

we request that the General Assembly appoint a special committee to study and recommend, to the 189th General Assembly (1977), *definitive guidance* (emphasis mine).[7]

b. In the same month the Advisory Council on Church and Society voted to place the issue of homosexuality on its docket of studies.[8]

The executive Committee of the Council prepared "A Prospectus for Study" which was revised and adopted by the Advisory Council on January 28, 1976. It began immediately to prepare by collecting resource materials and "names of persons who could serve well on such a task force."[9]

2. The Advisory Council on Church and Society developed a "Prospectus for Study" and an "Advice and Counsel Memorandum" which it brought to the Assembly. The memorandum was passed out by an official representative of the Council to the original subcommittee responsible for initial responses to the overtures regarding homosexuality, with the appeal that the study not be done through the Stated Clerk's office, but that it instead be done through the Advisory Council on Church and Society.[10]

This document was then passed out to the total Bills and Overtures Committee at the outset of their deliberations on the subcommittee's report.[11]

The chairperson of the Advisory Council further explained the Memorandum and the process by which the Council would proceed if given the task. *She admitted the credibility gap*, but said there are checks and balances and that the study could proceed with no special funding if done through the Advisory Council on Church and Society.[12]

3. Members of the Advisory Council on Church and Society not only made their request known at each of

those crucial times but then continued to speak on *numerous occasions* during the hours of the Committee's deliberation, even after the chairperson had clearly stated on three occasions there would be no further input from outside the Committee unless requested. Input from the Council was often requested, but it was not limited to those times.

At this time the Committee discussed who should appoint the task force and was leaning toward the Moderator of the General Assembly. The chairperson of the Advisory Council on Church and Society and a representative of its executive committee were asked to speak to that point by the chairperson of Bills and Overtures with no resistance from the Committee.

The representative of the executive committee spoke first. "The Moderator has no staff. The office of the Stated Clerk would have to staff the Moderator's appointments. *We know we have a credibility problem.* That's built into our task. We are the church's lightening rod. *There is no agency which really wants to deal with this matter, including Church and Society,* but we will do it because we think it is our job."[13]

It seemed strange that persons not wanting to tackle this job were working so hard to get the assignment.

The chairperson of the Advisory Council then added: "I never make appointments without consulting many people. I would welcome the help of the Moderator. I could guarantee that both of us would have veto power on any appointment to the committee."[14]

Further discussion dealt with numerous aspects of the total report when they again discussed *who should appoint the task force.* The chairperson of

Bills and Overtures told the Committee that Jeanne Marshall and Moderator Adair had given their commitment that both would have full veto power over task force membership. Much debate followed and strong sentiment against the wisdom of having Church and Society lead the study was expressed by a number of people.[15]

Eldon Berry spoke out: "The way Church and Society set up its task force is the wrong way. They have a bias that I don't like. If they proceed in the direction they've been going since 1970, then I don't want them. The committee should be composed of church persons. They can consult the experts."[16] Janet Penfield spoke in agreement.

Then the chairperson of the Advisory Council was asked to speak again to clarify the status of the study proposed by the Council. This was the fifth time that Church and Society people had spoken regarding the study, in addition to the request to hand out the Memorandum and to the report that the Moderator and chairperson of the Advisory Council were willing to appoint the task force. That makes seven specific references to the "Memorandum," five of which were after the committee had already decided there would be no further input from outside the Bills and Overtures Committee.

The chairperson of the Advisory Council then spoke as to why the study had not proceeded further and responded as to why their Prospectus and Memorandum did not allow for wider theological representation. The Committee overwhelmingly voted twenty to six to have a broad-based committee of church persons who could consult with experts rather than have experts in theology and sexuality do the study. (I will let you decide if that clear mandate was followed.)

They then voted on who ought to appoint the task force. The vote was between the Moderator and the Stated Clerk's staff or the Moderator and chairperson of the Advisory Council on Church and Society using Church and Society staff. The vote was very close.

At that point, a representative of the Advisory Council "erupted from the chairs behind the committee table: 'Our Church and Society mandates require expertise! I think you've chosen against the Church and Society process, unless the General Assembly changes our mandate.' "[17]

The Committee was surprised and shocked. The chairperson led them to discuss the former action again. Then another vote was taken in the light of the outburst. This time the vote on how the task force should be appointed was:

1. Moderator with consultation and staff from the Stated Clerk (ten votes).
2. Moderator and Church and Society chairperson with staff from Church and Society (sixteen votes).

I had just watched over a three-day period one of the most carefully planned and orchestrated efforts at direct and unhealthy influence that I have ever seen and I had to remain silent while the Advisory Council on Church and Society was giving continual input. It was painful. I just watched it. When the representative "erupted" from behind the chairs to finally win the day because nothing else had worked, I wanted to shout. I wanted to stand up and speak to the Committee and tell them what I had observed. I wanted to describe the process I had watched and how such unwholesome tactics could be extremely destructive in the church. The process had not been good.

Both persons from the Advisory Council admitted the credibility gap.[18]

Members of the Bills and Overtures Committee also spoke to that credibility gap shortly before they voted.

" 'There are members and ministers who, if they see it is from Church and Society on a document, throw it in the wastebasket.' "[19]

"Conrad Massa noted: 'The implication is that with Church and Society staff it will be a different kind of report than if it is a committee appointed by the Moderator.' "[20]

"Samuel Crothers interjected: 'I think there will be very little difference in the outcome, but a great difference in how well people will receive it.' "[21]

"Joe Pound said: 'If people in the church distrust Church and Society, we ought to do something about that. Can the Moderator use the staff of Church and Society?' "[22]

This was obviously a genuine concern within the committee. I shared those convictions.

Again, I want to say, for a council that didn't want to lead the study, it had a strange way of proving it.

If these deliberations had not been written down and put in print by Dr. Jack Rogers, I would never have shared these thoughts because they could not have been substantiated. Dr. Rogers was one of two official General Assembly theologians and he followed these deliberations carefully. He had no thought of how those facts would be useful in helping clarify what has happened.

4. The General Assembly Task Force on Homosexuality was appointed by Jeanne Marshall and Thelma Adair. We assume they both had veto power. They were carrying out the mandate of the General Assembly. The report from that task force is now in.

The task force voted fourteen to five in favor of the ordination of homosexuals and that the homosexual lifestyle can be a viable Christian lifestyle.

In contrast to their recommendations, the official Presbyterian Panel survey requested by the task force in January, 1977, found that over seventy percent of the pastors, elders, and lay people believe it would not be proper or judicious to ordain such persons and over ninety percent of these groups surveyed said they believe their congregations would not accept such a person as pastor. (See figure 1 in Appendix 2) Again, I say, the task force was not truly representative of the church. The fears expressed by members of the Bills and Overtures Committee have been realized.

The make-up of the task force really represents the make-up of the Advisory Council on Church and Society. What is my evidence? Remember the vote within the task force: fourteen to five. Now read the vote within the Advisory Council on Church and Society in sending the recommendation with support for the majority report to the Assembly: fifteen to three.

I believe my thesis is established.

Why am I including this material in this book? Not because I am angry. I thank God that He has healed me of that, although it took a long time. I include it for three reasons. *First*, this style of leadership is dangerous to the well-being of our church and the church needs to know about it so they can do something about it. It has been suggested that members of the Council are not serving as advisors. They are serving as a political lobbying group that is highly skilled and committed to taking the church where they want it to go. This is both dangerous and un-Presbyterian, because we believe in the parity of the ministry. It is also *very divisive*. The divisiveness caused by the Council is not only a result of the issues it raises and the answers it gives, but also of the methods it uses.

Second, I include this Appendix because our church is not the only denomination in which this kind of thing is happening. People in all mainline churches need to be aware of the possibility of such tactics, and to learn how to stand up to them with firmness.

Third, I wanted to puncture the myth that momentum is on the side of the majority report.

May I remind you that less than thirty persons have thus far voted in favor of the majority report. May I also remind you of what the Presbyterian Panel's survey revealed just last year. We are now learning what numerous sessions and presbyteries are saying from all over the country.

The momentum is *not* on their side. Nor will it be at the General Assembly. I hope that members of the Advisory Council on Church and Society will not have the privilege of continually speaking to their recommendation on the floor of the Assembly as they did in the Committee. The time has come when others are going to have to speak. We need to hear from the church itself.

This also needs to be true in all General Assembly Committees.

In 1977 I visited many different committees at the Assembly to listen to their deliberations. Again, I attended the Bills and Overtures Committee and found representatives of the Advisory Council on Church and Society not just listening, but participating strongly. I also found this happening in three other important committees.

Finally, out of frustration I confronted the chairperson of the Advisory Council on Church and Society and asked why everywhere I turned I found Church and Society staff and/or members monitoring the committees and giving guidance; sometimes rather strong guidance. Her response was, "That is our mandate. We are called to give guidance to General Assembly Committees." Is that the proper role for the Advisory Council on Church and Society? Was that the intention when restructuring took place a few years ago? Is it true to the parity of the ministry? Is it not, in fact, much more hierarchical in nature?

I served for four years on the Council on Discipleship and Worship. We never functioned that way. Our assignment was to be a listening post to the church, not to be determining ahead of time where the church should go and then planning strategies of how to move her there.

The commissioners who were representing their presbyteries from all over the country were the ones called to make the decisions.

When people, who seem to have official authority, give suggestions or recommendations and forceful outbursts, how can others within the church better express their *true* convictions?

What is the role of the national staff? To be servants of the church. What is the role of the Advisory Council on Church and Society? To be servants of the church. The church is the people. How can we help our leadership to be more sensitive and responsive to the people whom they represent and to heal the obvious cleavage in the church?

The majority and minority reports call for us to overcome homophobia, an unnatural fear and revulsion of homosexuals. They are right in calling us to face up to those sins of fear, revulsion, and hostility. But church power-plays produce far more homophobia toward the gay liberation movement, both inside and outside the church, than any other thing that could have been done.

There is a crisis of confidence in the General Assembly. We have struggled with that for nearly twenty years. During those years the denomination has lost nearly one-third of its members. Often there has been a significant gap between the actions of the General Assembly and the hearts of our people.

The Presbyterian Panel's survey on this issue (see Chapter 2) revealed a serious gap between the national staff, clergy in special ministries, and the lay people and pastors serving in local churches. The gap is too great— greater right now than ever in my ministry!

The General Assembly needs to fulfill both a pastoral role and a prophetic role. Lately, it has not been doing either.

We need to find ways to help the General Assembly and our national staff be more responsive to where the church is—what "people in the pew" believe. Or, we need to change leadership.

Appendix 2.
A Survey on Homosexuality*

	Members	Elders	Pastors	Retired Ministers	National Staff
Do you believe it might ever be judicious and proper for a presbytery to ordain to the professional ministry a person who engages in homosexual activities?					
no, never	45%	51%	39%	52%	12%
no, probably not	26%	26%	29%	25%	27%
yes, probably	14%	12%	20%	9%	32%
yes	4%	4%	10%	8%	19%
no opinion/don't know	7%	3%	2%	1%	3%
no response	5%	4%	1%	5%	7%
Do you believe that your congregation would accept as its pastor, associate or assistant pastor a qualified person who engages in homosexual activities?					
no, never	60%	68%	67%	65%	27%
no, probably not	30%	24%	29%	22%	46%
yes, probably	1%	2%	1%	1%	8%
yes	+	–	+	–	7%
no opinion/don't know	4%	3%	1%	5%	7%
no response	4%	3%	1%	6%	5%
Would you accept as your pastor a person who engages in homosexual activities?					
no, never	55%	64%	43%	71%	22%
no, probably not	25%	19%	30%	14%	30%
yes, possibly	6%	6%	13%	8%	24%
yes	4%	2%	8%	4%	14%
no opinion/don't know	6%	4%	6%	–	5%
no response	4%	3%	1%	4%	5%

*Presbyterian Panel Survey on Homosexuality and Related Issues, prepared by the Research Division of the Support Agency, UPCUSA, SA-RD/MCM-3/March 1977, questions 7a,c,e, p. 68.

Notes

Chapter 1. Gay Rights Go To Church

[1]Roy Birchard, "Metropolitan Community Church," *Foundations: Baptist Journal of History and Theology* (April-June, 1977), pp. 127–28.

Chapter 2. Deadlines and Dominoes

[1]Tracy Early, "The Struggle In The Denominations: Shall Gays Be Ordained?," *Christianity and Crisis*, May 30 and June 13, 1977, p. 121.

[2]Excerpt of Bishop Paul Moore's statement to the Episcopal Church's House of Bishops, October 3, 1977, Port St. Lucie, Florida.

[3]"Bishops Say Ordination of Homosexuals Inadmissible," *Diocesan Press Service*, No. 77325 (October 3, 1977), p. 1.

[4]Excerpt of statement by Bishop John M. Krumm, endorsed also by the Standing Committee of the Diocese of Southern Ohio, February 8, 1977.

[5]Early, "The Struggle," p. 119.

[6]"Part III, Social Principles," *The Book of Discipline of the United Methodist Church* (Nashville, 1976), para. 71D, p. 90.

[7]News release on the Task Force Study on Homosexuality,

Majority and Minority Report, *Background...*, January 23, 1978, p. 1.

[8]*Ibid.*, p. 3.

[9]*Ibid.*, p. 3.

[10]*Ibid.*, p. 6.

[11]The *Presbyterian Panel* is an ongoing series of mail surveys undertaken several times a year. The 3,669 persons who agreed to participate 1976-1978 included members (about 100 from each synod except Puerto Rico), elders (about 50 from each synod), and pastors (about 50 from each synod). Other clergy, staff, and missionaries are also included. This particular survey on "Homosexuality and Related Issues" was sent to panelists in January, 1977, and summarized March, 1977. The survey was done at the request of the Task Force on Homosexuality in keeping with the directive of the General Assembly to study Christian approaches to homosexuality. Sixty-four separate questions were asked. For response format see Appendix 2, page 175.

[12]"Chicago Presbytery Opposes Homosexuality," *The Presbyterian Layman*, vol. 11, no. 1 (January 1978), p. 1. (Reprint from *Chicago Daily News*, Dec. 14, 1977).

[13]*Ibid.*, p. 1.

[14]"The Church And Homosexuality: A Preliminary Study," issued in 1977 by the Stated Clerk of the General Assembly, Presbyterian Church in the U.S., para. F, p. 2.

[15]Early, "The Struggle," p. 121.

[16]*Ibid.*, p. 121.

[17]John J. McNeill, *The Church and the Homosexual* (Kansas City, 1976), Preface and Introduction.

Chapter 3. Our Valley of Decision

[1]Donald Williams, *Homosexuality, the Bible, and the Church* (Los Angeles, 1978), p. 7.

[2]Jerry R. Kirk, "The Bible, The Presbyterian Church And Homosexuality: Pastor's Perspective, *Bell Tower News* (College Hill Presbyterian Church periodical), vol. 24, no. 2 (February, 1978), pp. 1–2.

Chapter 4. The Real Crisis—God's Rights

[1]*The Constitution of the United Presbyterian Church in the United States of America, Part II, Book of Order,* 1977-78, Ministers—para. 49.044; Ruling Elders—para. 47.074.

Chapter 5. Text and Context

[1]Ben Patterson, "A Belated Answer," *The Wittenberg Door,* n.d.

[2]*Ibid.*

[3]Williams, *Homosexuality, the Bible, and the Church,* p. 53.

[4]*Ibid.,* p. 55.

[5]Also discussed in Everett F. Harrison, "The Biblical Teaching On Homosexuality," unpublished. Harrison is Professor Emeritus of New Testament, Fuller Seminary.

[6]Derrick S. Bailey, *Homosexuality And The Western Christian Tradition* (Hamden, Conn., 1975), p. 4.

[7]McNeill, *The Church And The Homosexual,* p. 47.

[8]David L. Bartlett, "A Biblical Perspective on Homosexuality," *Foundations: Baptist Journal of History and Theology* (April-June, 1977), p. 134.

[9]Williams, *Homosexuality, the Bible, and the Church.*

[10]Bartleti, "Biblical Perspective on Homosexuality," p. 137.

[11]Williams, *Homosexuality, the Bible, and the Church*, p. 70.

[12]Bartlett, "Biblical Perspective on Homosexuality," p. 140.

[13]John M. Batteau, "Sexual Differences: A Cultural Convention?", *Christianity Today* (July 8, 1977), p. 9.

Chapter 6. Fathers Know Best

[1]News Release, Task Force Homosexual Study, p. 3.

[2]*Confessions of St. Augustine.*

[3]Addition to the Report of the Assembly Committee on Bills and Overtures to the 188th General Assembly (1976), May 24, 1976, report 3, p. 1.

[4]"The Confession of 1967," *The Constitution of the United Presbyterian Church in the United States of America, Part I, Book of Confessions* (Philadelphia, 1970), para. 9.27, 9.29.

[5]*Ibid.*, para. 8.04.

[6]*Ibid.*, para. 6.004.

[7]*Ibid.*, para. 6.006.

[8]*Ibid.*, para. 6.009.

[9]Edward A. Dowey, Jr., *A Commentary On The Confession of 1967 And An Introduction to "The Book of Confessions"* (Philadelphia, 1968), p. 201.

[10]*Book of Confessions*, para. 5.001-5.002.

[11]Martin Luther, *Works*, vol. 25 (St. Louis, 1972), p. 164.

[12]News Release, Task Force Homosexual Study, p. 3.

Chapter 7. Sloppy Agape or Liberating Love

[1]John Calvin, *Commentary on 1 Corinthians*, trans. John W. Fraser (Grand Rapids, 1960), pp. 124–25. For this citation and the one from Calvin's Commentary on 1 Corinthians, I am indebted to Dr. Richard Lovelace's book *The Church and Homosexuality* to be published in June 1978 by Revell.

[2]C. S. Lewis, *The Problem of Pain* (New York, 1974), pp. 45-48.

Chapter 8. Clinics and Clerics: Medical and Psychological Research

[1]Arno Karlen, *Sexuality and Homosexuality: A New View* (New York, 1971), p. 186.

[2]*Ibid.*

[3]John Money, "Sexual Dimorphism and Homosexual Gender Identity," *Psychological Bulletin*, vol. 74 (b) (Dec. 1970), pp. 435–40.

[4]Jim Kasper and Mike Bresse, "Former Homosexuals Speak Out," audio tape of a conference on homosexuality, Atlanta, Georgia, 1977.

[5]Irving Bieber, *et.al.*, *Homosexuality: A Psychoanalytical Study* (New York, 1962) p. 220.

[6]Dr. Richard Lovelace, Dr. Donald Williams, and Dr. Aahmes Overton, "Minority Report", tape transcript, PUBC meeting, Chicago O'Hare Hilton, February 13, 1978, no. HC-A and B. Available from Thompson Media, Stahlstown, Pennsylvania 15687.

[7]C. A. Tripp, *The Homosexual Matrix*, (New York, 1975), p. 12.

[8]Irving Bieber, *et.al.*, "Conclusions," ed. Joseph A. McCaffrey, *The Homosexual Dialectic* (Englewood Cliffs, N.J., 1972), p. 86.

[9]McNeill, *The Church and the Homosexual*, pp. 7, 11

[10]Edmund Bergler, *Homosexuality: Disease or Way of Life?* (New York, 1956), p. 7.

[11]David Lester, *Unusual Sexual Behavior* (Springfield, Ill., 1975), p. 231.

[12]*Ibid.*, p. 227.

[13]Helmut Thielicke, *The Ethics of Sex* (New York, 1964), p. 3.

[14]Robert R. Carkhuff, *Helping and Human Relations*, vol. 1 (New York, 1969), p. 5.

[15]James Mallory, M.D., and Robert Neuremberger, Ph.D., an audio-taped interview in Atlanta, Georgia, May, 1977.

Chapter 9. Gay Agony: The Real Paradox

[1]Flanders Dunbar, M.D., *Mind and Body: Psychosomatic Medicine* (New York, 1947).

[2]"Please Hear What I'm Saying" (abbreviated version), author unknown.

[3]"Episcopal priest Malcolm Boyd emerges from shadow to sunlight," *Contact,* Official newsletter of Evangelicals Concerned, Inc., vol. 1, no. 5, September 1976, pp. 1, 4.

[4]Chris Glaser, "A Newly Revealed Christian Experience," *Church & Society/Homosexuality: Resources for Reflection,* May-June, 1977, p. 11.

[5]*Ibid.*, p. 11.

[6]Norman Pittenger, "The Homosexual Expression of Love,"

Is Gay Good?, ed. W. D. Oberholtzer (Philadelphia, 1971), pp. 233–34.

⁷Lewis Williams, "Walls of Ice—Theology and Social Policy," *Is Gay Good?* ed. W. D. Oberholtzer (Philadelphia, 1971), pp. 163 ff.

Chapter 10. Hope For The Homosexual

¹"O For A Thousand Tongues to Sing" (1739).

Chapter 12. How to Effect Change: Mobilization

¹Richard C. Halverson, *Perspective*, Washington, November 9, 1977.

²Author unknown.

³Quote by Vic Jamieson in a paper delivered at the first meeting of the newly established Advisory Council on Discipleship and Worship in 1972.

Chapter 13. Love That Lasts—A Reconciling Community

¹Frank Worthen, address, February 13, 1978, Chicago, Illinois.

²Howard Snyder, *The Problem of Wineskins* (Downers Grove, Ill., 1975); and *The Community of the King* (Downers Grove, Ill., 1977.)

³Ronald R. Rand, *How to Equip Lay People to Evangelize Regularly*, College Hill Presbyterian Church, Fraternity Printing, Cincinnati, Ohio, 1974.

⁴Gary R. Sweeten, "The Development of a Systematic Human Relations Training Program for Evangelical Christians," (Ed.D. diss.) University of Cincinnati (1975). See also Carkhuff, *Helping and Human Relations*, Vol. 1.

[5]Sweeten, "Training Program for Evangelical Christians." See also Gary R. Sweeten, "The Integration of Helping Professionals and The Local Church," Christian Association for Psychological Studies, 1975, Santa Barbara, California; and Richard W. Walters, *The Amity Book*, 4986 Fuller Avenue S. E., Kentwood, Michigan 49508.

[6]Marshall Ginsberg, M.D., "Oh, God! or Oh, Freud!" Address at Conference of Clergy and Mental Health Professionals, January, 1978, Cincinnati, Ohio.

[7]*Ibid.*

[8]Betty Tapscott, *Inner Healing Through Healing of Memories*, 1977, Box 19827, Houston, Texas 77024. See also Ruth C. Stapleton, *The Experience of Inner Healing* (Waco, Texas, 1977); and Dennis Linn and Matthew Linn, *Healing of Memories*, (New York, 1974).

[9]Gary R. Sweeten, "Specific Christian Interventions and Helping Techniques" (1978).

OTHER HELPS

Intentional Communities: Graham, Pulkingham; *They Left Their Nets* (Morehouse Barlow, New York, 1973).

Specific ministries to Homosexuals:
a. Jesus Outreach Center, 704 Country Club Road, Fairmount, W. Va. 26554
b. Love in Action, Box 265, San Rafael, Calif. 94902
c. Exit Ministries, Melody Land Christian Center, Anaheim, Calif. (714-778-1000) (Hot Line)

A paper on Ministry to Homosexuals
Christian Marriage Enrichment
Marriage and Family Newsletter
Vol. II, Number 6, June/July 1976.

Appendix 1. For Presbyterians Only

[1]Minutes of the 182nd General Assembly of the UPCUSA, Part I, Journal (Philadelphia, 1970), pp. 802, 888.

[2]*Ibid.*, pp. 918–19.

[3]*Ibid.*, pp. 904–06.

[4]*Ibid.*, p. 889.

[5]*Ibid.*, p. 469.

[6]*Ibid.*, p. 469.

[7]Jack Rogers, "Should The United Presbyterian Church Ordain Homosexuals?" (Cambridge, Mass., 1976), Exhibit B (New York Presbytery Overture).

[8]*Ibid.*, Exhibit I (Advice and Counsel Memorandum), p. 1.

[9]*Ibid.*, p. 2.

[10]Rogers, "Ordain Homosexuals?", p. 8.

[11]*Ibid.*, p. 10.

[12]*Ibid.*, p. 12.

[13]*Ibid.*, p. 18.

[14]*Ibid.*, p. 18.

[15]*Ibid.*, pp. 20–21.

[16]*Ibid.*, p. 21.

[17]*Ibid.*, p. 22.

[18]*Ibid,* pp. 12, 18.

[19]*Ibid.*, p. 21.

[20]*Ibid.*, pp. 21–22.

[21]*Ibid.*, p. 21.

[22] *Ibid.*, p. 21.

Bibliography

Articles

Bartlett, David L. "A Biblical Perspective on Homosexuality," *Foundations: Baptist Journal of History and Theology* (April-June, 1977), 133–47.

Birchard, Roy. "Metropolitan Community Church," *Foundations: Baptist Journal of History and Theology* (April-June, 1977), 127–32.

Early, Tracy. "The Struggle in the Denominations: Shall Gays Be Ordained?", *Christianity and Crisis* (New York: Christianity and Crisis, Inc., May 30 and June 13, 1977), 118–22.

"Episcopal Priest Malcolm Boyd emerges from shadow to sunlight," *Contact*, vol. I, no. 5 (Miami, Florida: Evangelicals Concerned, Inc., September, 1976).

Glaser, Chris. "A Newly Revealed Christian Experience," *Church & Society/Homosexuality: Resources for Reflection* (New York: Church & Society, UPCUSA, May-June, 1977).

Pittenger, Norman. "The Homosexual Expression of Love," *Is Gay Good?* ed. W. D. Oberholtzer (Philadelphia: The Westminster Press, 1971) 221–38.

Williams, Lewis. "Walls of Ice—Theology and Social Policy," *Is Gay Good?* ed. W. D. Oberholtzer (Philadelphia: The Westminster Press, 1971) 163–84.

Books

Bailey, Derrick S. *Homosexuality And The Western Christian Tradition* (Hamden: The Shoe String Press, Inc., 1975).

Bergler, Edmund. *Homosexuality: Disease or Way of Life?* (New York: Collier Books, 1956).

Bieber, Irving, et. al. *Homosexuality: A Psychoanalytical Study* (New York: Vintage Books, 1962).

Bieber, Irving, et. al. "Conclusions," in Joseph A. McCaffrey, ed. *The Homosexual Dialectic* (Englewood Cliffs, N.J.: Prentice Hall, Inc., 1972).

Bucke, Emory Stevens, ed. *The Book of Discipline Of The United Methodist Church* (Nashville: The United Methodist Publishing House, 1976).

Calvin, John. *Commentary on I Corinthians*, trans. John W. Fraser (Grand Rapids: Eerdmans, 1960).

Carkhuff, Robert R. *Helping and Human Relations*, Vol. I (New York: Holt, Rhinehart & Winston, 1969).

The Constitution of the United Presbyterian Church in the United States of America, Part I, Book of Confessions, 2nd ed. (New York: The Office of the General Assembly, UPCUSA, 1970).

The Constitution of the United Presbyterian Church in the United States of America, Part II, Book of Order, 1977-78 (New York: The Office of the General Assembly, UPCUSA, 1977).

Dowey, Edward A., Jr. *A Commentary On The Confession of 1967 And An Introduction To "The Book of Confessions"* (Philadelphia: The Westminster Press, 1968).

Dunbar, Flanders, M.D. *Mind and Body: Psychosomatic Medicine* (New York: Random House, 1947).

Karlen, Arno. *Sexuality and Homosexuality: A New View* (New York: W. W. Norton & Co., 1971).

Kinsey, Alfred C., Pomeroy, Wardell B. and Martin, Clyde E. *Sexual Behavior In The Human Male* (Philadelphia: W. B. Saunders Co., 1948).

Lester, David. *Unusual Sexual Behavior* (Springfield, Illinois: Charles C. Thomas, 1975).

Lewis, C. S. *The Problem of Pain* (New York: Macmillan Paperbacks, 1974).

Linn, Dennis and Linn, Matthew. *Healing of Memories* (New York: Paulist Press, 1974).

Luther, Martin. *Works*, Vol. 25 (St. Louis: Concordia Publishing House, 1972).

McNeill, John J. *The Church and the Homosexual* (Kansas City: Sheed Andrews and McMeel, Inc., 1976).

Minutes of the 182nd General Assembly of the UPCUSA, Part I, Journal (Philadelphia: Office of the General Assembly, UPCUSA, 1970).

Rand, Ronald R. *How to Equip Lay People to Evangelize Regularly* (Cincinnati: College Hill Presbyterian Church, 1974).

Snyder, Howard. *The Problem of Wineskins* (Downers Grove: Inter-Varsity Press, 1975); *Community of the King* (Downers Grove: Inter-Varsity Press, 1977).

Stapleton, Ruth C. *The Experience of Inner Healing* (Waco, Texas: Word Books, 1977).

Tapscott, Betty. *Inner Healing Through Healing of Memories*, 1977, Box 19827, Houston, Texas 77024.

Thielicke, Helmut. *The Ethics of Sex* (New York: Harper & Row, 1964).

Tripp, C. A. *The Homosexual Matrix* (New York: McGraw-Hill Book Co., 1975).

Walters, Richard W. *The Amity Book*, 4986 Fuller Ave., S. E. Kentwood, Mich. 49508.

Williams, Donald. *Homosexuality, the Bible, and the Church* (Los Angeles: BIM Publishing Co., 1978).

Periodicals

"Chicago Presbytery Opposes Homosexuality," *The Presbyterian Layman,* vol. 11, no. 1 (New York: The Presbyterian Lay Committee, January, 1978).

Kirk, Jerry R. "The Bible, The Presbyterian Church And Homosexuality: Pastor's Perspective," *Bell Tower News*, vol. 24, no. 2 (Cincinnati: College Hill Presbyterian Church periodical, February, 1978).

Patterson, Ben. "A Belated Answer," *The Wittenberg Door*, n.d.

Pamphlets

"The Church and Homosexuality: A Preliminary Study," issued by the Stated Clerk of the General Assembly, Presbyterian Church in the U.S., 1977.

Papers

Ginsberg, Marshall, M.D. "Oh, God! or Oh, Freud!," address at Conference of Clergy and Mental Health Professionals, January, 1978, Cincinnati, Ohio.

Harrison, Everett F. "The Biblical Teaching On Homosexuality," unpublished.

Rogers, Jack. "Should The United Presbyterian Church Ordain Homosexuals?" (Cambridge, Mass.: The Case Study Institute, 1976).

Sweeten, Gary R. *The Development of a Systematic Human*

Relations Training Program For Evangelical Christians,
Ed.D. dissertation, University of Cincinnati, 1975.

Sweeten, Gary R. "The Integration of Helping Professionals and
The Local Church," paper delivered at the Christian Association for Psychological Studies, 1975, Santa Barbara, California.

Sweeten, Gary R. "Specific Christian Interventions and Helping Techniques" (1978).

Press Releases

"Bishops Say Ordination of Homosexuals Inadmissable,"
Diocesian Press Service, no. 77325, (New York, October 3,
1977).

Money, John. "Sexual Dimorphism and Homosexual Gender
Identity," Psychological Bulletin, 1970 (Dec.) vol. 74(b)
425–40.

"News Release on the Task Force Study on Homosexuality,
Majority and Minority Report," *Background . . .* , (New York:
Division of Communications, UPCUSA, January 23, 1978).

Survey

"Presbyterian Panel Survey on Homosexuality and Related Issues," SA-RD/MCM-3 (New York: Research Division of the
Support Agency, UPCUSA, March 1977).

Tapes

Kasper, Jim and Bresse, Mike. *Former Homosexuals Speak Out,*
audio tape of a conference on homosexuality, Atlanta, Georgia, 1977.

Lovelace, Dr. Richard, Williams, Dr. Donald and Overton, Dr.
Aahmes. "Minority Report," tape transcript, PUBC meeting,
Chicago O'Hare Hilton, February 13, 1978, no. HC-A and B.
Available from Thompson Media, Stahlstown, Pa. 15687.

Mallory, James, M.D. and Neuremberger, Robert, Ph.D., an
audio taped interview in Atlanta, Georgia, May, 1977.

The essence of this book's message can be heard on these tapes by Jerry Kirk:

1. "The Bible, the Presbyterian Church and Homo-sexuality"—$3.95

2. "The Homosexual Crisis and the Mainline Church"
   A Time to Speak
   A Time to Learn
   A Time for Hope
   A Time for Action
   Set of four one-hour tapes—$14.95

Tapes on church renewal:

1. Renewal of the Local Congregation." Set of two tapes—$9.95

2. "God Cares for Me"—$2.50
   "God Takes Sin Seriously"—$2.50
   "God Loves Sinners"—$2.50
   "God Loves Other Sinners through Me" (1 & 2)—$2.50

Tapes may be ordered from:

College Hill Presbyterian Church
5742 Hamilton Avenue
Cincinnati, Ohio 45224